Some Concepts and
Consequences of the
Theory of Government
and Binding

Linguistic Inquiry Monographs
Samuel Jay Keyser, general editor

Some Concepts and
Consequences of the
Theory of Government
and Binding

Noam Chomsky

The MIT Press
Cambridge, Massachusetts
London, England

This book is partly based on a talk by Noam Chomsky before the Sixth
Scandinavian Conference of Linguistics in Røros, Norway, June 19–21,
1981. It was meant to be written out as a paper to appear in the proceedings
of that conference, but as it developed into a book only part of which is
directly related to the original Røros talk, it is now published as a separate
monograph. The other papers of the conference are published in *Papers
from the Sixth Scandinavian Conference of Linguistics*, edited by Thorstein
Fretheim and Lars Hellan, Tapir Publishers, University of Trondheim,
N-7055 Dragvoll, Norway.

Fourth printing, 1988

This book was set in VIP Times Roman by Village Typographers, Inc.,
and printed and bound by Halliday Lithograph Corporation in the United
States of America.

Library of Congress Cataloging in Publication Data

Chomsky, Noam.
  Some concepts and consequences of the theory of government and binding.
  (Linguistic inquiry monographs ; 6)
  Bibliography: p.
  1. Government (Grammar). 2. Generative grammar. I. Title.
II. Series.
P299.G68C5   415   82–7218
ISBN 0–262–03090–X   AACR2
     0–262–53042–2 (pbk.)

Contents

Series Foreword

We are pleased to present this monograph as the sixth in the series *Linguistic Inquiry Monographs*. These monographs will present new and original research beyond the scope of the article, and we hope they will benefit our field by bringing to it perspectives that will stimulate further research and insight.

Originally published in limited edition, the *Linguistic Inquiry Monograph* series is now available on a much wider scale. This change is due to the great interest engendered by the series and the needs of a growing readership. The editors wish to thank the readers for their support and welcome suggestions about future directions the series might take.

Samuel Jay Keyser
for the Editorial Board

Some Concepts and Consequences of the Theory of Government and Binding

Introductory Comments

I would like to sketch some features of an approach to linguistic theory that has been slowly coming into focus in the past few years and that has considerable promise, I believe.[1] Because of the crucial roles played by the notions of government and binding, the approach is sometimes called *government–binding (GB) theory*. I will refer to it by that name here, though it develops directly and without a radical break from earlier work in transformational generative grammar, in particular, from research that falls within the framework of the Extended Standard Theory (EST).

The concepts and principles of GB theory are fairly simple, and it should be possible to present an elementary and systematic exposition of them, presupposing very little. I have not undertaken that task here. Rather, the presentation is more exploratory, with successive revisions as the discussion proceeds.

As concepts and principles become simpler, argument and inference tend to become more complex—a consequence that is naturally very much to be welcomed. We hope that it will ultimately be possible to derive complex properties of particular natural languages, and even to determine the full core grammar of a language with all of its empirical consequences, by setting the parameters of general linguistic theory (universal grammar, UG) in one of the permissible ways. While this goal should always have been an obvious one, it is only quite recently that the task could actually be considered in a serious way, a development that is in my opinion a sign of significant progress in linguistic theory. I will discuss some examples, particularly in section 4, where certain fairly complex phenomena that have recently been described are derived from some basic and simple principles of GB theory, with a variety of consequences—and, as should be anticipated, a variety of problems, some previously unnoticed, that resist solution. Section 1 is devoted to a noticeable and I think significant shift in focus in recent work from the study of rule systems to the study of subsystems of principles, a consequence of the rather considerable success in reducing the variety of potential grammars consistent with empirical data from certain well-studied languages. Section 2 deals with the properties of various types of empty categories—NP-trace, PRO, and variables—as determined by the principles of GB theory. In section 3, a different perspective toward the same problem is introduced which permits the reduction of empty categories to variants of a single notion. Section 4 applies these conclusions to a specific domain of linguistic fact. In section 5, the character and typology of empty categories are reconsidered from a still different and I think more principled point of view, leading to some suggestions concerning the so-called pro-drop parameter and other related matters.

1. The Variety of Rule Systems

Two perspectives can be distinguished in the study of grammar, one which emphasizes rule systems and the other, systems of principles. Consider, for example, recent versions of EST. The rule system consists of three basic parts:

(1)
(A) Lexicon
(B) Syntax: (i) Base component
            (ii) Transformational component
(C) Interpretive components: (i) PF component
                          (ii) LF component

The lexicon specifies the inherent properties of lexical items. In particular, it determines what I will call the θ-*marking* properties of lexical items that serve as heads of constructions; for example, the verb *persuade* has the property that it assigns a certain *thematic role* (θ-*role*) to each category for which it is subcategorized, its object and clausal complement, and indirectly to its subject. I assume that θ-marking of the subject is mediated through the verb phrase of which the verb is the head, perhaps determined compositionally. In addition, the lexicon specifies properties of phonetic form and meaning that are not determined by rule.

The rules of the base component generate *D-structures* ("deep structures"), which we may think of as representations in configurational terms of the *grammatical functions* (subject, object, etc.; henceforth, GFs) that are associated with θ-roles. Of the GF positions (henceforth, *A-positions*—what have sometimes been called *argument positions*), all and only those that are assigned θ-roles (θ-*positions*) are lexically filled at D-structure, namely, with elements bearing these θ-roles, including as one option the phonetically null element PRO.

The rules of the transformational component assign to each D-structure an associated *S-structure* in which GFs are once again configurationally defined. In S-structure, however, an element bearing a θ-role may appear in a position assigned no θ-role (a $\bar{\theta}$-*position*). Thus, the S-structure associated with sentence (2a) is (2b), in which *John* is the subject but the subject position bears no θ-role:[2]

(2)
a. John was persuaded to leave
b. [$_{NP_i}$ John] was persuaded e_i [PRO$_i$ to leave]

Here the pair ([$_{NP_i}$ *John*], e_i) constitutes a *chain*, the second term being the *trace* of the first. The chain is assigned a θ-role by virtue of the fact that one of its members (namely the trace) occupies a θ-position. PRO stands for an element bearing an independent θ-role, hence base-generated in place in (2b); it is coindexed with the object of *persuade* (an object control verb) by the theory of control. The S-structure (2b) is formed from the corresponding D-structure by application of the rule Move α, which moves *John* from the object position (a θ-position) to the $\bar{\theta}$-position of matrix subject, leaving a trace coindexed with its antecedent by convention. The S-structure (2b) contains two chains, one consisting of *John* and its trace, the other consisting merely of PRO. Each chain is assigned a θ-role.

I will say little about the interpretive components here. The PF component maps S-structure to a surface structure in phonetic representation, and the LF component maps S-structure to a representation in LF (read "logical form", with familiar provisos). These are some of the basic properties of the system outlined in (1).

A second perspective from which one can view grammatical processes focuses on principles that hold of rules and representations of various sorts. These principles fall into the following subsystems, which I will discuss in turn.

(3)
a. X-bar theory
b. θ-theory
c. Case theory
d. Binding theory
e. Bounding theory
f. Control theory
g. Government theory

X-bar theory is familiar in several variants; I will adopt one without further comment in discussion below.

A basic principle of *θ-theory* is the θ-*Criterion,* which states that each term of LF that requires a θ-role (each *argument*) is assigned a θ-role uniquely, and that each θ-role determined by lexical properties of a head is uniquely assigned to an argument. If θ-roles are assigned to chains, as suggested above, then the θ-Criterion must be reformulated in the obvious way in terms of chains and their members.

The theory of *Case*[3] is concerned with the assignment of (abstract) Case to elements that are in Case-marking positions (for example, objects of prepositions and transitive verbs, subjects of tensed sentences). One basic principle is J.-R. Vergnaud's *Case Filter,* which states that every NP with phonological content must receive Case. Case too can be thought of as being assigned to chains, in the obvious way. The presence of Case makes elements "visible" to the application of certain rules, both rules of the phonological component and the LF rules that assign θ-roles to chains. Pursuing this idea, one can largely (perhaps completely) reduce the Case Filter to the θ-Criterion. See Chomsky (1981a, chapter 6), Stowell (1981).

The theory of *binding* is concerned with the relations of anaphors and pronominals to their antecedents, if any. It deals with the phenomena that fall under the Specified Subject Condition (SSC) and Nominative Island Condition (NIC) of earlier work (see Chomsky (1980a)).

The theory of *bounding* specifies locality conditions, in particular, the *Subjacency Condition* on movement rules.

The theory of *control* is concerned with the choice of antecedents for PRO.

The theory of *government* contains such principles as the *Empty Category Principle* (ECP), which states that each trace must be "properly governed", a narrower concept than government. Richard Kayne has provided evidence that the ECP applies at the level of LF representation (see Kayne (1979), also (1981a)). While certain questions remain open, I think the weight of evidence currently suggests that the binding theory applies at the S-structure level.[4] The concept of government plays a central unifying role throughout the system. Thus, θ-role and Case are assigned under government.[5]

These systems of principles interact in a variety of ways, and certain relations also obtain between the subtheories of (3) and the subsystems of rules in (1). A fully articulated theory of universal grammar (UG) will develop the properties of these systems and the relations that hold among them. I will sketch some of these properties and interconnections as we proceed. Each of the systems of (1) and (3) has associated with it certain parameters, which are set in terms of data presented to the person acquiring a particular language. The grammar of a language can be regarded as a particular set of values for these parameters, while the overall system of rules, principles, and parameters is UG, which we may take to be one element of human biological endowment, namely, the "language faculty".[6]

One key question is, How much of the rule system must actually be specified in a particular grammar? Or equivalently, What aspects of the rule system must actually be learned, as knowledge of language is acquired? Or again equivalently, What is the actual set of parameters associated with the rule system (1), and how freely can they be assigned values? For familiar reasons, we want the choice of values for parameters to be as limited as possible, so as to maximize the explanatory power of linguistic theory and to account for the possibility of acquiring knowledge of grammar ("language learning"). Much of the research over the past 20 years within the general outlines of the theory of transformational generative grammar has been devoted to narrowing the range of possible alternatives consistent with available data concerning certain well-studied languages.[7] In the course of this work, there has been a gradual shift of focus from the study of rule systems, which have increasingly been regarded as impoverished (as we would hope to be the case), to the study of systems of principles, which appear to occupy a much more central position in determining the character and variety of possible human languages. Let us now consider this question, reviewing in turn the components of (1).

Consider first the lexicon (1A). For each lexical item, the grammar must indicate those properties that are idiosyncratic, undetermined by general principles of UG. For example, the grammar of English must specify that *persuade* is a verb having a particular form, meaning, set of complements, and way of θ-marking its complements and (indirectly) its subject, if any. A large part of "language learning" is a matter of determining, from presented data, the elements of the lexicon and their properties. Standard "poverty of stimulus" arguments indicate that the structure of the lexicon itself must be predetermined to quite a substantial extent.

Turning next to the syntactic component of the grammar (1B), consider the base rules (1Bi). These must suffice to determine (for English) the D-structure underlying (2b), for example. In earlier work, it was assumed that this D-structure is determined by rewriting rules of the base, among them (4a,b):[8]

(4)
a. S $\rightarrow$ NP INFL VP
b. VP $\rightarrow$ V NP S'

We now ask how much of (4) must actually be specified in the grammar.

The fact that the head of VP in (4b) is V need not be specified, since this fact follows from X-bar theory (3a). Therefore, (4b) can at least be simplified to (5):

(5)
VP $\rightarrow$ Head NP S'

However, (5) too is redundant as a base rule, since it in part recapitulates information presented in the lexicon, namely, that there is a verb *persuade* which takes an NP object and a clausal complement. Noting this fact, let us propose a very general principle, the *Projection Principle,* which states informally that the θ-marking properties of each lexical item must be represented categorially at each syntactic level: at LF, S-structure, and D-structure. For LF, the Projection Principle expresses in a particular notation something that is true virtually as a matter of definition. Extended to S-structure, the Projection Principle has among its consequences the basic elements of what has been called *trace theory*. Extended further to D-structure, the Projection Principle expresses the idea that D-structure is a "pure" representation of *thematically relevant GFs* (henceforth, GF-θ). Properly formulated, the Projection Principle extends the θ-Criterion from LF to S-structure and D-structure. One consequence is that movement rules (i.e. Move α) must transport an element to a $\bar{\theta}$-position. For example, if an argument is moved from a θ-position in D-structure to a second θ-position in S-structure, the associated chain will be assigned θ-role twice, violating the θ-Criterion; if an argument is moved from a $\bar{\theta}$-position in D-structure to a θ-position in S-structure, then the θ-Criterion will be violated at D-structure though it is satisfied at S-structure; and so forth. This is a basic property of Move α, to which we will return.

By the Projection Principle, the S-structure of (2a) must be something like (2b), and the corresponding D-structure must be essentially the same, with *John* in the position of its trace and the matrix subject position unfilled. We can thus further reduce rule (5): the complements of the Head need not be specified, since they are determined by the lexicon, under the Projection Principle. We are now supposing D-structure to have two correlated properties: (i) it is abstracted from S-structure by the transformational rules and therefore contains no traces; (ii) it is a "pure" representation of GF-θ. Note that X-bar theory is closely related to the Projection Principle in the sense that the complements of a head in the realization of an X-bar expansion need not be stipulated, given this principle.

What remains of (4b) is the order of constituents in (5). However, even this is quite possibly a redundant specification in part. It is plausible to suppose that Case theory involves an adjacency requirement, at least as one of the unmarked options, with English adopting a particularly strict variant (consider, for instance, **I have read often these books*). Since the verb must assign Case to its object by the Case Filter, the object must be adjacent to the verb, accounting for part of the linear order in (5).[9] What now remains of the base rule (4b), then, is the stipulation that the Head is initial in VP in English, just as N, A, and P are initial in the categories projected from them under X-bar theory, a general property of English.

To account for (2), we must also provide for the fact expressed in the rule (4a) that each of the clausal constituents—the matrix and embedded clauses—has a subject. It might be thought that this follows from the Projection Principle, since both verbs θ-mark their subjects, but this is not quite correct. While subcategorized complements are obligatory for heads, the θ-marked subject is not, as we can see from passives or nominals (for example, (2) or *the belief that S*). Furthermore, nonarguments can occupy the subject position, as in *it is clear that S, I expect* [*it to be clear that S*]; in fact, the subject position *must* be filled by a pleonastic element in structures lacking a θ-marked subject. It seems, then, that the requirement that a clause have a subject position is independent of the Projection Principle. We may think of it instead as a general principle governing D-structures, hence also governing structures derived from them. There are good reasons, which I will not elaborate here, to assume that the same is true of languages that appear to allow a "missing subject" (for instance, the Romance languages other than French).

The Projection Principle and the requirement that clauses have subjects are conceptually quite closely related. In fact, we may stipulate that a lexical element that θ-marks its subject position (e.g. *persuade* but not *seem*) does so if and only if the position is filled, that is, in clauses but only optionally in NPs. (Note that passive morphology eliminates the two correlated properties of θ-marking the subject and of Case-marking an object.) I will henceforth refer to the Projection Principle along with the requirement that clauses have subjects as the *Extended Projection Principle*.

Another feature of the grammar of English that must be specified is that English is "configurational" in the sense that the GFs are represented in formal structures, as in (2). Possibly configurationality is a property of subsystems of grammar rather than of grammars; it may also be related to parameters of Case theory. For discussion of this parameter within the framework assumed here, see Chomsky (1981a, chapter 2).

Summarizing, it seems that the base component for English consists of the specification of a limited variety of parameters: [+configurational], "Head first", subject–VP order, etc.; and an elaboration of language-specific idiosyncrasies, such as properties of complex nominal expressions. How many of the latter can be reduced to general principles remains an open and relatively unexplored question. In some cases, at least, this clearly should be possible.

Consider, for example, such ungrammatical NPs as (6):

(6)

*[all some men]

Clearly, it should be unnecessary to account for (6) by particular rules of English grammar, either base rules or specification of parameters. We do not expect to find that the equivalent will be grammatical in some other language. A natural assumption is that (6) is barred by a general principle of LF to the effect that each operator must bind a distinct variable. If so, then no rules of particular grammar exclude (6); in fact, it should be freely generated by the base rules and "filtered out" at LF.

Note that the principle in question is not one of logic. It is an uninteresting notational question in standard systems of logic whether to permit vacuous quantification or to rule it out by a condition on the well-formedness of expressions. However, the principle is a perfectly reasonable one as an empirical condition on the syntax of LF in natural languages, as part of UG. Apart from excluding such structures as (6), the same principle will bar (7) while permitting such NPs as (8):

(7)

a. *the man [who John saw Bill]
b. *the man [who$_i$ John saw him$_j$] $(i \neq j)$
c. *who did John see Bill
d. *I wonder who John saw Bill

(8)

a. the man [who John saw t]
b. the man [who$_i$ John saw him$_i$]
c. the man [who$_i$ they think that if Mary marries him$_i$, then everyone will be happy]
d. I wonder [who$_i$ they think that if Mary marries him$_i$, then everyone will be happy]

In (8a), t is the trace of *who* and is, by definition, a variable bound by *who,* so that the phrase is understood in the following way:

(9)

the man x such that John saw x

In (8b), *him* may be understood as a variable under the resumptive pronoun strategy. This strategy is marginal in standard English, though it is found in other languages and is fairly common in colloquial English in such structures as (8c,d), where bounding theory prohibits *Wh* Movement.

We do not want to rule out such structures as (8b–d) and others like them by rules of grammar. In fact, we do not want the syntax to exclude any of the structures of (7), (8). Rather, (7) is barred and (8) permitted by the requirement that an operator at LF must bind a variable, and languages or dialects may differ as to how this variable is realized; pronouns can serve as variables because they need not have independent reference. Apart from the barrier to vacuous operators, the theory of grammar should contain no special devices to deal with the examples of (7), (8). Introducing additional special devices to establish the distinction between (7) and (8) is simply a defect of any theory of grammar that resorts to it, since the same result already follows from more general considerations.

Later, we will see that there is good reason to suppose that the barrier to vacuous operators should be strengthened to the requirement that there also cannot be "free variables", in a sense to be explained; see the discussion of (40) in section 2. It has also been proposed that the requirement that each operator bind a distinct variable in LF be strengthened to the *Bijection Principle,* which stipulates that each operator must bind one and only one variable, thus accounting for "weak crossover" violations as in (10) and for the marginal status of (11):[10]

(10)
his mother loves everyone   (in the sense: for each person x, x's mother loves x)

(11)
who did you give a picture of t to t

We return to this question. Whether this extension is warranted in general or in part, the weaker principle—barring vacuous operators and free variables in the sense to be explained—seems quite well motivated and eliminates some of the necessity for specific base rules.

Is it necessary to stipulate a principle barring vacuous operators as a component of UG governing the syntax of LF, or could the principle be reduced to still more basic considerations? Suppose, for example, that it were argued that examples such as (6) and (7) that violate this principle simply "make no sense". If this option is pursued, it will be necessary to explain why they make no sense. Thus, consider (7). Many languages fairly freely allow left-dislocation structures in which the element in topic position is related to no gap or pronoun in the associated clause, though some weaker "aboutness" relation holds between the clause and the topic. It is not obvious why the same could not be true of relative clause constructions. Or suppose that vacuous quantification were permitted in such cases as (6) and (7). It is easy enough to devise a system of logic in which vacuous quantifiers are permitted in well-formed expressions, but simply ignored in interpretation. Why should the same not be true of natural language, so that, for example, (7c) would mean 'Did John see Bill?' or perhaps 'John saw Bill'. There is no a priori argument against such possibilities. If they are not realized, it is presumably because some principle concerning the syntax of LF—an empirical principle of UG—precludes them.

In part at least the barrier to vacuous operators might be reducible to other considerations. Consider the resumptive pronoun strategy. Normally, this involves no overt operator in COMP, contrary to (8b,c). The question then arises whether there is an empty operator in COMP binding the resumptive pronoun in this case, or no operator at all. Suppose that the latter is correct. Suppose further that such examples as (8c) in colloquial English are dismissed as some kind of analogic form. Then we might interpret relative clause constructions with resumptive pronouns as involving an operation of predication, the relative clause being regarded as an open sentence predicated of the head. Suppose, furthermore, that this is a general property of relative clause interpretation, whatever the internal structure of the relative clause.[11] This assumption would suffice to bar (7a), and by pursuing its implications further we might derive the barrier to vacuous operators in relative clauses quite generally.

Pursuing the general line of reasoning we have been considering, we conclude that the variety of base grammars is very limited; in fact, there is only a finite number of such grammars, and a relatively small number. Each such grammar consists simply of the specification of values for parameters such as those discussed, along with a restricted variety of peripheral (noncore) phenomena, which must be specifically learned. X-bar theory, the Extended Projection Principle, and other principles will then determine the class of D-structures, given the lexicon and the specification of these parameters.

We might still say that there is a base phrase structure grammar, say, a context-free grammar, which generates D-structures (or, for that matter, S-structures or LF), but it is derivative; it need not be specified or learned, but derives from deeper principles and the specification of parameters that constitutes the actual grammar. Its status is comparable to that of a system of rules that might be derived from a grammar to specify the class of rhyming pairs. More generally, the concept "language" itself, however one wants to define it (if at all), is derivative and epiphenomenal, like the class of rhyming pairs. Language, whatever it may be, is a notion more abstract than grammar, more remote from actual mechanisms, consequently raising new problems which may or may not be worth trying to solve (personally, I am skeptical). The concepts of phrase structure grammar were quite natural insofar as their role was understood to be that of determining the phrase markers of (base) grammatical structures. However, these devices are surely not appropriate for the specification of such parameters as those just noted, and with the development of X-bar theory and other principles of the sort we have been considering, it should be clear that the theory of phrase structure grammar has no standing as a component of UG.

If, in fact, phrase structure grammars do not exist as a component of UG but are merely an artifact, we can return to a question discussed in the earliest work in transformational generative grammar, namely, whether phrase markers have the formal properties represented in conventional tree diagrams, and if so, why. The question can be raised, of course, only if we have some independent notion of phrase structure. Suppose, then, that we adopt the set theoretic approach to phrase markers (and in general, level markers) of Chomsky (1955), much refined and improved in Lasnik and Kupin (1977). In the earliest work, it was assumed that at the level of D-structure, phrase markers can be expressed as tree structures because they are base-generated by a phrase structure grammar, but that this might not be true at surface structure, and considerable attention was devoted to the conditions under which it would be true. Reopening the question from our present viewpoint, we note first that the concept "base-generation" has no clear meaning. D-structures, S-structures, and other representations are determined by fixing parameters of UG, and the same is true of the derivations in which they are associated. (I will nevertheless continue to use the term for expository purposes, referring to elements as "base-generated" in their D-structure positions.) Still, we can ask whether D-structures, S-structures, etc., have the properties of tree structures. Insofar as they are determined by X-bar theory, this will be the case. But there are other factors that enter into determining their properties. Reanalysis and restructuring processes, for instance, may yield phrase markers that cannot be represented as tree structures. Some examples will be discussed below. Furthermore, X-bar theory can be constructed so that it does not require that phrase markers have tree properties. It has occasionally been suggested that coordination might be understood in terms of union of phrase markers (in effect, three-dimensional trees with the conjuncts filling the same position in the associated two-dimensional projection), linear order being determined by a "spell-out" rule. The assumption would be, then, that if the very same language were to be used in a medium having a dimension in addition to linear time, this "spell-out" rule would be unnecessary. Such suggestions might be correct, and I think that they merit examination. Much more radical departures from tree structures can be, and sometimes have been, proposed. I will not explore these questions here, but merely note that incompatibility of such proposals with the theory of phrase structure grammar stands as no barrier to them.

Consider next the transformational component (1Bii). It has been proposed in recent work that this can be reduced—at least for core grammar—to the single rule Move α (that is, "move any category anywhere"), perhaps with certain parameters involving choice of α and landing sites in the sense of Baltin (1978). The principles of (3) will interact to determine where and how the rule Move α can apply. If so, then the class of syntactic components is finite and in fact extremely limited in variety.

Reducing the variety of possible grammars has been one of the major preoccupations of research in generative grammar during the past 20 years, motivated by the twin goals of enhancing explanatory power and providing the basis for an understanding of how knowledge of language can be attained. There has been some misunderstanding of this project and its achievements (in part fostered by misinterpretation of the results of mathematical linguistics, a matter that I will not explore further here).[12] Restricting the class of possible transformational rules has often been interpreted as reducing the role of grammatical transformations in grammar. A comparison of recent work with the investigations of, say, 20 to 25 years ago reveals a rather different picture. The scope of the rule Move α is not radically different from the scope of the variety of transformational rules developed in these earlier studies (though it is, of course, substantially narrower than the practice of generative semanticists during the period when this approach was under serious consideration). In some cases, the applicability of transformations has indeed been reduced (e.g. Agent Postposing in passives); in other cases, it has been extended (e.g. NP Raising, Verb Phrase Fronting in Romance). In general, though, the scope of transformational rules in recent studies is not strikingly different from what was assumed in the earliest research, the same work being done now by a much restricted rule inventory supplemented with general conditions on rule application and output. Along parallel lines, the variety of base systems has also been substantially reduced; clearly there would be no point in merely shifting the complexity and variety of grammars from one component to another. It has often been assumed that the natural outcome of these developments would be to eliminate the transformational component of the grammar completely. This would indeed be reasonable, if it did not lead to a corresponding or greater proliferation of base systems. Given the extreme simplicity of the transformational component as compared with the rich variety and complexity of base rules, however, a much more natural proposal would be to eliminate the rewriting rules of the base in favor of transformational rules (now, Move α) and the principles of the subsystems (3a–g). This appears to be a viable prospect, and a very welcome one.

With regard to the interpretive components of the grammar (1C), little need be said in the present context. These permit only limited, surely finite variability. With regard to the PF component (1Ci), the matter is uncontroversial, and the conclusion is implicit in existing theories of morphology and phonology. As for the LF component (1Cii), since direct evidence as to its character is extremely limited, it must be assumed that very little variation is possible among grammars, such differences as there are probably being a reflex of other aspects of grammar for which the language learner encounters overt evidence. (On this matter, see Horvath (1980), Huang (1980).)

The general conclusion toward which recent research has been tending is that rule systems are fairly rudimentary in character. The more interesting questions involve the systems of principles (3a–g), though certain important questions regarding the nature of rule systems remain open within this general framework. One such question concerns the nature of the relation between thematically relevant grammatical functions (GF-θ) and thematically empty grammatical functions (GF-$\bar{\theta}$) (for example, the relation between the GF-θ "object of *persuade*" and the GF-$\bar{\theta}$ "subject of *be persuaded* . . ." in (2)), and more generally the relation between D-structure (regarded now as a pure representation of GF-θ) and S-structure. One thesis of a strong form of transformational grammar is that this is the same relation as the one that holds between *wh*-phrases and the variables they bind, extraposed phrases and the positions in which they receive their interpretations, etc.; that is, that the relation in all of these cases is in essence Move α. I believe this thesis to be correct, for reasons to which I will return.

A second conclusion, which seems increasingly clear, is that there are only finitely many (in fact, relatively few) possible core grammars. The reasons for this conclusion should be fairly clear from the remarks already made, and they become evident when gaps are filled in. If this approach is on the right track, then we may assume that language learning (i.e. acquisition of knowledge of a particular grammar) is a matter of determining the values for a restricted number of parameters of the systems (1) and (3). The lexicon can presumably expand without limit in general (though some languages may have inherent restrictions that limit its scope), but this fact raises no substantial problems for the theory of language acquisition since the lexicon does not undergo explosive growth; each word must be learned, with some fixed amount of time and evidence. The same is true of noncore parts of grammar. This is not to deny, of course, that there are UG conditions on the character of the lexicon and the marked periphery of grammatical systems; on the contrary, there must be stringent conditions of this nature.

---

2. General Properties of Empty Categories

So far, I have been considering the question of how much of the rule system must actually be specified in a particular grammar, the answer apparently being: rather little. A second, obviously related question is, What is the nature of the various representations, namely, D-structure, S-structure, PF, and LF? One of the most interesting aspects of this topic involves the nature and distribution of gaps, which are sometimes called *empty categories* (ECs). If the Extended Projection Principle is correct, then (a) an EC is present wherever a θ-role is assigned but the corresponding θ-position contains no lexical material, and (b) the category S must always contain an EC as subject if no overt subject is present, as in infinitival clauses or finite clauses in pro-drop languages with missing or inverted subjects.[13] There are, I think, good reasons to believe that this assumption is correct, at least in the class of languages that have so far been seriously studied from the point of view I am considering.

One piece of evidence supporting this assumption has already been mentioned: if we adopt it, the distribution of pleonastic elements in non-pro-drop languages such as English can readily be explained, and the same appears to be true of their counterparts in languages that allow "missing subjects" (see Rizzi (1980b), Burzio (1981), Chomsky (1981a,b), among others). A more fundamental, though more intricate, reason is that gaps share properties of overt elements, namely, overt anaphors, pronominals, and R-expressions ("referential" expressions, such as names). For example, PRO with arbitrary variable-like interpretation, as in (12), appears only in the positions that are "transparent" in the sense of binding theory, that is, the positions in which overt anaphors need not be bound by an antecedent within the same major category (clause or NP; see note 16):

(12)
it is unclear [what PRO to do *t*]

This interpretation for a gap is possible for the subject of an infinitive or a gerund, but not for the subject of a tensed clause or a direct object, mirroring the properties of anaphors and pronouns with disjoint reference. The fact is easily explained if there is an actual EC PRO filling this position and sharing relevant properties of anaphors and pronominals, a conclusion that accords with the Extended Projection Principle and also simplifies (virtually trivializes) the relation of S-structure to LF in this respect. Similarly, gaps interpreted as variables (e.g. gaps bound by *wh*-phrases) share crucial properties of names, a fact that is also explained if the gap is actually occupied by an EC with name-like properties, again trivializing the relation of S-structure to LF. On other grounds, it would simply be an accident that gaps share crucial properties with overt elements that have a similar semantic role.

The relation between ECs and overt elements of various kinds is not superficially obvious, but it does appear to follow in a straightforward manner from the principles of the subsystems (3a–g), a fact that is, I believe, of considerable interest; it also lends important support to the Extended Projection Principle, which is in any event quite natural. In the remainder of this study, I would like to consider the validity of the assumption that the behavior of ECs mirrors that of overt elements, the apparent differences deriving from the principles of GB theory.

Apart from its implications with regard to the Extended Projection Principle and other related principles, the study of gaps is interesting for two basic reasons. First, it has proven to be an important probe into the nature of syntactic rules and representations, revealing many of their properties. Second, the properties of gaps are intrinsically significant in that the language learner can confront little direct evidence bearing on them, so that it is reasonable to assume that they reflect deeper principles of UG, the biologically determined endowment that will be the primary concern for those interested more in the nature of the human mind than in the arrangement of data in the environment.

Let us now consider more closely some of the central notions of GB theory, beginning with the concept of government, a modification of the traditional notion. For the purposes of this discussion, I will tentatively assume the following formulation:[14]

(13)

α *governs* β if $\alpha = X^0$ (in the sense of X-bar theory), α c-commands β, and β is not protected by a maximal projection.

We say that β is *protected* by a maximal projection if the latter includes β but not α. Assume VP to be the maximal projection of V and S' the maximal projection of INFL, and assume further the interpretation of the agreement element AGR of INFL as in note 8. Then the subject of a tensed clause (but nothing in the VP) is governed in D-structure by AGR, given (4a); the elements subcategorized by a verbal, nominal, or adjectival head are governed by the head; the object of a preposition is governed by the preposition; and the embedded subject of an infinitival construction is governed by an appropriate element in COMP (if present) or by the matrix verb or adjective in an Exceptional Case-marking construction such as (14), a raising construction such as (15), or a small clause such as (16), assuming deletion of the major category (i.e. S'-Deletion in (14) and (15)):[15]

(14)
John believes [Bill to be incompetent]

(15)
John seems [*t* to be incompetent]

(16)

John considers [Bill incompetent]

In general, Case-marking and θ-marking take place under government, as determined by inherent properties of the governor.

We define the *governing category* for α to be the minimal S or NP containing α and a governor of α.[16] In terms of this notion, we can formulate the basic principles of the theory of binding as follows:

(17)

Principles of the Theory of Binding
A. An anaphor is bound in its governing category.
B. A pronominal is free in its governing category.
C. An R-expression is free.

The terms *free* and *bound* are defined in the customary way, in terms of coindexing by a c-commanding category. More precisely, we interpret *bound* (similarly, *free*) in (17) as "locally A-bound", where β is A-*bound* by α if β is bound by α and α is in an A-position, that is, a position having a GF such as subject or object. The element β is $\bar{A}$-*bound* by α if it is bound by α and the latter is in an $\bar{A}$-position (a non-A-position), such as COMP. Thus, variables are $\bar{A}$-bound by their operators in COMP, but an NP-trace or anaphor is A-bound by its antecedent. The element β is "locally X-bound" by α if it is X-bound by α ($X = A$ or $\bar{A}$) and α is, in the obvious sense, the "closest" binder of β.[17]

Anaphors include overt categories such as *each other, himself,* and the ECs NP-trace and PRO. Pronominals are elements containing the features person, gender, number, and possibly Case, and an optional phonological matrix, excluding elements identified as nonpronominal lexical items (e.g. *each other, John*). Note that I am regarding PRO as a pronominal anaphor, as is rather natural; I will return to this question. R-expressions too may be either overt (e.g. *John*) or empty (namely, variables bound by an operator).

From Principle A we derive the essential content of the basic binding conditions SSC and NIC for anaphors; the same conditions on pronominals (determining disjoint reference in this case) are derived from Principle B. Principle C entails, for example, the results of (18):

(18)

a. *he_i thinks $John_i$ likes Bill
b. *who_i does he_i think t_i likes Bill

In (18a), we interpret coindexing as intended coreference, putting aside some interesting questions about the meaning of this notion; see Higginbotham (forthcoming). Example (18b) is the familiar case of (strong) crossover; it cannot be interpreted as 'for which person x, x thinks that x likes Bill', as the coindexing would require. The variable t_i in (18b) functions in the same manner as *John* in (18a) with respect to the binding theory. Correspondingly, variables are not subject to the SSC and NIC.

Since PRO is a pronominal anaphor, it is subject to Principles A and B of the binding theory, from which it follows that PRO lacks a governing category and is therefore ungoverned. This is the basic property of PRO, largely determining its distribution, both the respects in which this distribution is shared with anaphors and those in which it is not. As noted, the theory of government includes the Empty Category Principle (ECP), which stipulates that trace *must* be governed. In fact, a slightly stronger requirement of "proper government" must be imposed, leading us to formulate the *Extended ECP:* an EC is trace if and only if it is properly governed and PRO if and only if it is ungoverned.

Note the logical possibility of an EC that is a pure pronominal as distinct from the pronominal anaphor PRO. We will hold this possibility in abeyance until section 5.

Let us now consider the relations holding between gaps and overt elements. We will first classify gaps into several types and then examine them in turn.

(19)
a. Gaps with antecedents that lack an independent θ-role
    (i) and are locally A-bound
    (ii) and are locally Ā-bound
b. Gaps with antecedents that have an independent θ-role
c. Gaps having no antecedent

Under (19ai), we find examples such as (20a,b):

(20)
a. John is likely [t to win]
b. John was [killed t]

In (20), t is the trace of *John,* an EC A-bound by *John,* which is in a θ̄-position, lacking an independent θ-role; *John* "inherits" its θ-role from the θ-position of its trace, that is, it heads a chain assigned a θ-role in the manner already described. The examples (20a,b) are formally similar, respectively, to (21a,b), the latter having an overt category where the former exhibit an EC.

(21)
a. they want [each other to win]
b. they [killed each other]

(21a,b) differ from (20a,b) in several respects. First, the antecedent of the anaphor in (21) has an independent θ-role, which the antecedent in (20) lacks. Second, the overt anaphors of (21) have Case, as required by the Case Filter, whereas the corresponding ECs of (20) do not. (Recall that passives do not assign θ-role to the subject or Case to the object; in (21a), we may assume that a deleted complementizer *for* governs and assigns Case to the embedded subject. See below.) The similarities and differences between overt categories and ECs are accounted for by binding theory, Case theory, and θ-theory. Like overt anaphors, the gaps of (19ai) fall under Principle A of the binding theory and are therefore subject to the SSC and NIC. As already noted, it follows from the Projection Principle and the θ-Criterion that movement can only take place to a $\bar{\theta}$-position, the basic property of Move α.

Furthermore, the trace in (20) is properly governed, satisfying the ECP; structures such as (22a,b), in which the trace is not governed, are not possible:

(22)
a. *John is known [how [*t* to win]]
b. *John is probable [*t* to win]

The difference between *likely,* which induces S' Deletion and therefore government and raising, and *probable,* which does not, is a lexically marked idiosyncrasy, as the near synonymy of the examples indicates. The antecedent–trace relation of (19ai) also satisfies the Subjacency Condition of bounding theory, as (23) illustrates:

(23)
a. they$_i$ think [[PRO$_i$ to feed [each other]$_i$] would be difficult]
b. *they$_i$ seem [[t_i to feed [each other]$_i$] would be difficult]
c. they$_i$ think [[pictures of [each other]$_i$] will be on sale]

In (23a), the EC has an antecedent with an independent θ-role and is therefore PRO rather than trace. Though Subjacency is violated, nevertheless PRO and its antecedent can be coindexed, as is generally possible, irrespective of Subjacency, for anaphors apart from trace (cf. (23c)). In (23b), the antecedent of the EC is in a $\bar{\theta}$-position lacking an independent θ-role, so that the EC is trace. Subjacency is violated exactly as in (23a), but in this case the sentence is ungrammatical. Quite generally, Subjacency appears to be a property of the rule Move α, not of other coindexing relations. Note that (23b) in fact violates the ECP as well as Subjacency, so that it illustrates a double violation.

Summarizing, gaps of the type (19ai) are subject to Principle A of the binding theory and therefore satisfy the SSC and NIC; they are properly governed, satisfying the ECP; and they observe Subjacency.

Consider next examples of type (19aii), namely, variables. Variables fall under the category of R-expressions with respect to binding theory and are therefore subject only to Principle C; in short, their behavior is similar to that of the names for which they are "place holders". While this fact cannot be established a priori, it is natural enough. One example has already been cited, namely, the strong crossover case (18). To elaborate a bit further, consider the very similar example (24) and its interpretation (25):

(24)
which boy does he think [*t* will hurt himself]

(25)
for which boy *x,* he thinks [*x* will hurt *x*]

The variable must be present as an antecedent for the anaphor *himself;* otherwise, the latter will violate Principle A of the binding theory, since it must be bound in its clause (its governing category). Note that the trace *t* in (24) is not bound, and cannot be bound, by the subject that c-commands it, namely, *he;* if it were so bound, the interpretation would be (26):

(26)
for which boy *x, x* thinks [*x* will hurt *x*]

The interpretation (26) is semantically well formed; it is, in fact, a possible interpretation of (27):

(27)
which boy thinks [he will hurt himself]

However, (26) is not a possible interpretation of (24). Thus, variables are subject to Principle C of the binding theory, not Principle A, which would require that the variable be bound in S in (24). The behavior of variables as bound elements and as antecedents shows that they are in fact present at the level at which the binding theory operates, which I assume to be S-structure.

The S-structure corresponding to (27) is (28):

(28)
which boy [*t* thinks [he will hurt himself]]

Here, *t* is the variable bound by *which boy;* nothing prevents the pronominal *he* from being bound by *t,* since even if so bound, *he* is free in its governing category (the minimal clause in which it appears) and thus satisfies Principle B of the binding theory, which holds of pronominals.

Returning to (24), its interpretation (25) is parallel in form to (29a), not (29b):

(29)
a. he thinks [John will hurt himself]
b. he thinks [he will hurt himself]

In (29a), *John* is not bound by *he,* by Principle C of the binding theory. In (29b), however, the pronominal subject of the embedded clause, which is subject to Principle B of the binding theory, may be bound by the matrix subject; thus, (29b) is parallel to (28). The fact that the trace in (24) functions in the manner of the embedded subject of (29a), not (29b), provides evidence that variables are not pronominals. Since trace in (24) is free in its governing category S, it cannot be an anaphor. Thus, under the taxonomy induced by the binding theory, the variable is an R-expression, not an anaphor or a pronominal.[18]

Note further that variables, like NP-trace, must be properly governed; alongside (22), we find (30):

(30)
a. *who is it known [how [*t* to win]]
b. *who do you think [that [*t* won]]

Thus, variables fall under the ECP, which subsumes the *[*That*-Trace] Filter, as (30b) indicates.[19] Case (30a) might follow from another property of variables: as arguments they must receive θ-role, and θ-role assignment is contingent on Case under the Visibility Principle mentioned earlier. Thus, in part the ECP might be derivable from Case and θ-theory. (For discussion of this topic, with varying conclusions, see Borer (1981), Chomsky (1981a), Stowell (1981).) Furthermore, I believe that variables are subject to the Subjacency Principle, for reasons discussed elsewhere.[20]

Summarizing the properties of gaps with antecedents lacking independent θ-role (viz. (19a)): they are subject to Subjacency, are properly governed (subject to the ECP), and are anaphors if A-bound and R-expressions if $\overline{A}$-bound. The last property is consistent with their semantic interpretation.

Consider next the cases of (19b), namely, gaps with antecedents that have an independent θ-role, as in (31):

(31)
John told me [how [e to solve the problem (help myself)]]

Here e stands for the gap that serves as thematic subject of the embedded clause. The presence of the subject is determined by the Extended Projection Principle. The gap represented here as e is what we have been calling PRO, a pronominal anaphor. The pair (*John*, PRO) in (31) does not constitute a chain, since each of its terms is in a θ-position; chains are formed solely by Move α (but see the later discussion of (88), (89)). PRO in (31) is unlike the empty anaphor NP-trace and unlike the $\overline{A}$-bound variable in that it has an antecedent with an independent θ-role. The property that the antecedent (if any) has an independent θ-role is shared by PRO and overt pronouns, that is, all pronominals. At the same time, PRO is like an anaphor in that it has no specific independent reference.

In constructions in which either PRO or an overt pronoun is structurally possible, PRO is preferred by the Avoid Pronoun Principle, as in (32):

(32)
John likes [(his) winning the race]

In the position of subject of the embedded NP, an overt pronoun is possible because (genitive) Case is assigned in this position so that the Case Filter is satisfied. However, since this position is ungoverned, PRO is also possible.[21] In fact, the preferred interpretation for (32) with *his* present takes the pronoun to be disjoint in reference from the matrix subject, in accordance with the Avoid Pronoun Principle. The same principle suggests an approach to the interpretation of the "missing subject" of pro-drop languages; namely, that the subject is PRO, an option permitted when there is a "rich enough" inflection to determine the features of the missing subject.[22] (We conclude, therefore, that the subject position may be ungoverned in these languages.) The intuitive idea, then, would be that pronominals have phonological features only where they must, for some reason.

Since PRO is ungoverned, it cannot appear in such structures as (33a,b):

(33)
a. John wants [Bill to like PRO]
b. John thinks [PRO will win]

Compare (32) with (34):

(34)
*John likes [PRO book]

In (32), the subject of the object NP may be PRO, but in (34) it may not. The natural conclusion, then, is that the subject position is ungoverned in (32), but governed in (34); that is, the N *book* which is the head of N' and NP in (34) governs its subject, but the V *win* which is the head of the VP *winning the race* does not govern its subject in (32). This result will follow, as Dominique Sportiche and Youssef Aoun (to whom the observation is due) point out, if we modify the definition of government suggested above, requiring that the governor and the governed term share all maximal projections, VP being a maximal projection but not N'. See note 14. We achieve the same result if we understand *c-command* in (13) (the definition of *govern*) in something like the extended sense of Reinhart (1976); then *book* c-commands (hence governs) its subject in (34), NP being a projection of N, but *win* does not c-command its subject in (32), NP not being a projection of V (recall that we have taken INFL to be the head of S, VP being a maximal projection).[23]

Unlike trace, PRO does not appear to be subject to Subjacency, as (23a–c) or such sentences as (35a,b) illustrate:

(35)

a. they think [John said [that $\begin{Bmatrix} \text{[PRO to feed each other]} \\ \text{[PRO feeding each other]} \end{Bmatrix}$ would be

difficult]]

b. we feel [that $\begin{Bmatrix} \text{[PRO learning to cooperate]} \\ \text{[PRO helping each other]} \end{Bmatrix}$ is important for their

development]

In both (35a) and (35b), the antecedent of PRO is *they* (*their*), and PRO is not subjacent to the antecedent.[24] Also, the relation of *they* to PRO in (35a) violates the SSC in that PRO need not be bound by the "nearest" c-commanding subject, namely, *John*. Recall, however, that as a pronominal anaphor PRO is subject to both Principle A and Principle B of the binding theory, and though the SSC follows from each, it does not follow from their conjunction; rather, what follows from their conjunction is that PRO is ungoverned, from which it follows in turn that PRO is subject to the SSC in certain instances (e.g. (33a)) but not others. Thus, the binding theory determines crucial respects in which the distribution of PRO is similar to and differs from that of anaphors. Like other anaphors, PRO is excluded from the subject position of a finite clause (the NIC), but can appear in the transparent position of subject of infinitive and gerund. Unlike anaphors, PRO is restricted to these positions,[25] while *each other*, NP-trace, etc., can appear in complement position if there is an antecedent in the same clause or NP. PRO admits "long-distance control" violating Subjacency and the SSC (but see note 24). In the latter respect, PRO is unlike all other anaphors; in the former, it is like anaphors apart from trace, though as noted the theory of control does impose certain "locality conditions" on the relation of PRO to its antecedent. There is a good deal more to say about this topic, but I will leave it here. (See Chomsky (1981a, chapter 2) for further discussion of the theory of control.)

Summarizing the properties of gaps with antecedents that have an independent θ-role (namely, (19b)): they are ungoverned and are not subject to Subjacency, but rather to the principles of the theory of control.

Consider finally the third category of gaps, those lacking an antecedent (i.e. (19c)), as in (36):

(36)
it is clear [how [*e* to solve the problem]]

Here the gap e is like a pronoun in that it lacks an antecedent and like an anaphor in that it has no inherent reference; its interpretation is more or less that of a free variable, not a freely referring definite pronoun. (On the interpretation of arbitrary PRO, see Chomsky (1981a, chapter 6) and (1981b).) Again, we assume that this gap is PRO, a pronominal anaphor. As such, it is ungoverned; bounding properties are irrelevant, since there is no antecedent.

Summarizing finally, gaps have the following properties. The gaps of (19a), with an antecedent lacking a θ-role, are traces formed by Move α, either anaphors or variables depending on whether they are locally A-bound or Ā-bound, and correspondingly subject to Principles A or C of the binding theory, respectively. The gaps of (19b) and (19c), having either an antecedent with an independent θ-role or no antecedent, are PRO, a pronominal anaphor, subject to Principles A and B of the binding theory, hence ungoverned. Subjacency is a property of Move α, though control theory imposes other locality conditions on PRO. The two options for PRO—having or lacking an antecedent—are exactly those of pronouns, and PRO is also like pronouns in that its antecedent (if any) has an independent θ-role; but PRO is unlike pronouns, and like anaphors, in that it has no independent reference (but see note 22). The fact that trace is distinguished from PRO in terms of the character of its antecedent (if any) follows in a principled way from the Projection Principle and the θ-Criterion, which require that movement be to a θ̄-position, as noted earlier; and of course the fact that trace always has an antecedent follows from Move α (see below, however, for a qualification in the case of trace not c-commanded by its antecedent). In short, binding theory, Case theory, government theory (namely, the ECP), and bounding theory interact to determine the similarities and differences of distribution among gaps and overt elements of various kinds. Though the properties of these various elements are fairly complex in surface forms, the principles that determine them are quite simple and well motivated. Crucially, the properties of the several types of gaps, as well as the properties of anaphors, pronominals, and R-expressions having gaps as antecedents,[26] follow from the assumption that the gaps, while missing in surface structure at the PF level, are actually present (as ECs) at S-structure and LF. This provides strong support for the Extended Projection Principle, which requires the presence of ECs of the various types we have been discussing.

Let us now consider some more complex properties of ECs, which again support these basic principles of GB theory. Compare PRO and overt anaphors such as *each other*. Note that they share distribution at a certain level of abstraction; namely, both appear as subject of infinitives and gerunds. However, the two are in complementary distribution in these constructions in actual sentences, as illustrated in (37):[27]

(37)

a. they believe [$\left\{\begin{array}{l}\text{*PRO} \\ \text{each other}\end{array}\right\}$ to be intelligent]

b. they know how [$\left\{\begin{array}{l}\text{PRO} \\ \text{*each other}\end{array}\right\}$ to solve the problem]

The natural conclusion from these observations is that two theories interact to yield the distribution of PRO and overt anaphors. Their shared distribution at an appropriate level of abstraction is determined by binding theory, while their complementary distribution in actual sentences is determined by Case theory, that is, by the Case Filter, which holds of overt elements but not ECs. This is a typical example of the modularity of the systems of principles in (3a–g).

Note that the complementary distribution of PRO and *each other* is true only at a certain level of abstraction; it does not hold at surface structure, as we see from (38):

(38)
a. they want [PRO to win]
b. they want [each other to win]

At the level of S-structure, the corresponding forms are (39a,b):

(39)
a. they want [PRO to win]
b. they want [for [each other to win]]

The complementizer *for* is optionally present in D-structure and, if present, governs and assigns Case to the embedded subject, while excluding the possibility of (necessarily ungoverned) PRO. Optionality of *for* is a marginal property of English, yielding the apparent contrast of (38). At the appropriate level of abstraction (S-structure in this case), the complementary distribution predicted by Case theory holds.[28] What we should say, then, is that at the level of abstraction represented at S-structure, we find complementary distribution of *each other* and PRO, while at a higher level of abstraction (namely, one at which we identify such constructions as infinitival clause, gerund, etc.), the two elements share crucial distributional properties. As is often the case, the phenomena observed at surface structure may be uninformative and misleading in themselves, the more significant properties appearing only at a more abstract level as explained by the principles that determine the character of these more abstract levels of representation.

The properties of overt anaphors and PRO just discussed again provide indirect but significant support for the Extended Projection Principle. That is, we want a principled explanation for the fact that from one perspective gaps that function as anaphors share distributional properties of overt anaphors, though from another perspective they are in complementary distribution with overt anaphors (abstracting from the optionality of complementizers that disguises the latter property at surface structure). The explanation is provided by the principles of binding and Case theory, on the assumption that gaps appear where required by the Extended Projection Principle.

Consider next such constructions as (40a,b):

(40)
a. the men are too stubborn to talk to Bill
b. the men are too stubborn to talk to

By the Extended Projection Principle, the corresponding S-structures are (41a,b), where *e*, as before, is some EC.

(41)
a. the men are too stubborn [e_1 to talk to Bill]
b. the men are too stubborn [e_2 to talk to e_3]

The interpretation of these sentences makes it clear that e_1 and e_2 are PRO; e_1 is bound by *the men*, while e_2 lacks an antecedent and has the arbitrary variable-like interpretation of PRO in (36). That is, the interpretations are respectively analogous to (42a,b):

(42)
a. the men are so stubborn that they (the men) will not talk to Bill
b. the men are so stubborn that no one will talk to them (the men)

Our task is to determine the reason for this, and the nature of e_3.

Let us first consider the second of these questions, the nature of e_3. Since it is governed, it cannot be PRO. Therefore, it is trace. It cannot be the trace of e_2, because the latter is in a θ-position. Note that if the bracketed phrase were to be replaced, for example, by e_2 *to be talked to* e_3, so that e_2 is in a $\bar{\theta}$-position, then the structure reduces to (41a) with e_2 = PRO bound by *the men*. Furthermore, e_3 cannot be locally A-bound by *the men,* or it will be an NP-trace violating the binding theory. Therefore, it must be a variable. That is, is must be $\bar{A}$-bound by an operator O. The actual S-structure of (40b), then, must be (43):

(43)
the men are too stubborn [$_{S'}$ O_3 [$_S$ e_2 to talk to e_3]]

The operator O is an EC and is semantically empty, unlike a *wh*-phrase for example. Therefore, e_3 is in effect a free variable, assigned no range by its operator, in the embedded clause. But this violates natural requirements at LF, requirements that are in fact more or less complementary to the previously discussed principle barring vacuous operators. Suppose, then, that we supplement the principle barring vacuous operators by the requirement that each LF variable either be assigned a range by its operator or be assigned a value by an antecedent that A-binds it. It follows that e_3 must be bound by *the men,* though it is not locally bound by *the men* (rather, by O) and is not the trace of *the men.* As (42b) indicates, this is indeed the interpretation of e_3. The value of the variable e_3 is the referent of the matrix subject *the men.* Notice, however, that this conclusion requires that "free" in the formulation of Principle C of the binding theory be understood as "locally free" or, more precisely, "locally A-free", as indicated below (17). That is, we understand Principle C as in (44):

(44)
An R-expression must be A-free in the domain of the operator that $\bar{A}$-binds it.

This refinement has no effect apart from variables, and it is natural for variables.

Since e_3 is a variable $\bar{A}$-bound by O, the S-structure (43) must have been derived by application of Move α from the D-structure (45):

(45)
the men are too stubborn [$_{S'}$ COMP [$_S$ e_2 to talk to O]]

Therefore, the gap e_3 must satisfy island conditions that follow from Subjacency, along with other conditions that follow from the assumption that movement is involved in these constructions. This is in fact the case, as discussed in Chomsky (1977; 1980a, appendix; 1980b). Therefore, the relation of O to e_3 in (43) is indeed a case of Move α. Formal and semantic considerations converge on this conclusion, which is the only one consistent with the binding theory.

We have thus determined the status of e_3. Consider now the last open question: why is e_2 = PRO understood as having the arbitrary interpretation of free PRO rather than as being controlled by the matrix subject, as e_1 is in a similar configuration? Suppose, in fact, that e_2 is coindexed with the matrix subject *the men*, as e_1 is. Since *the men* is coindexed with e_3, as we have just seen, it follows that e_2 and e_3 are coindexed, violating Principle C of the binding theory, namely, (44). Therefore, e_2 cannot be coindexed with the matrix subject but must rather be uncontrolled PRO, with the arbitrary variable-like interpretation indicated in (42b). Thus, all properties of (40b) follow from the binding theory, given the constraint against free variables, a result that supports the Extended Projection Principle and the independent properties of Move α. This example and others like it are interesting in that it is highly implausible to suppose that relevant information about the interpretation might be available to every speaker who understands (40b) as (42b). It can only be supposed, then, that independent principles determine the interpretation.

One might propose that the relation of e_3 to *the men* in (43) is to be accounted for not by the barrier against free variables but rather by the stipulation that in such constructions the embedded clause, regarded as an open sentence, is predicated of the matrix subject in the manner discussed briefly in note 11. This is not correct, however. The embedded clause need not contain a gap or pronoun related to a matrix clause antecedent in these constructions, as Howard Lasnik points out; consider, for example, such sentences as *the coach is too incompetent for the team to win any games.*

It seems, then, that the barrier to vacuous operators should be supplemented by the requirement that variables at LF must either be assigned a range or a value by an antecedent and in this sense cannot be "free". Note again that these are not principles of logic, but rather empirical principles concerning the syntax of LF, hence, derivatively, the semantic interpretation of sentences.

One might think of relating the principle that operators must bind variables and that variables cannot be "free" to the Bijection Principle, but as Dominique Sportiche observes, this would be a dubious move, since the Bijection Principle imposes much weaker conditions than the other two.

Let us consider more closely the rule Move α, which we now assume to constitute the transformational component of the syntax (1Bii), with certain parameters. Considering the syntactic rule Move α abstractly, we see from the preceding discussion that it has the following basic properties:

(46)

Move α is the relation between an antecedent and a gap where:

a. the antecedent lacks an independent θ-role (and is therefore in a $\bar{\theta}$-position)

b. the gap is properly governed (if it is trace (see (48)))

c. the relation is subject to bounding theory (Subjacency)

We may tentatively take the characterization (46) to be, in effect, the definition of the syntactic rule Move α, returning to additional properties below. Note further that we can readily understand (46) in a still more theory-neutral way, interpreting the concept "gap" more abstractly. For example, any theory will somehow have to explain the fact that in the sentence *John was killed, John* is assigned the θ-role that *kill* assigns to its direct object in . . . *kill John,* and that the passive participle in this case does not have a direct object in the position of the associated active form. The "missing position" in the passive construction can then be taken as the "gap" in the sense of (46), whether one thinks of it as an EC in our terms or as not present at any level of representation. Either way, it is a question of fact whether (46) holds of the antecedent–gap relation, and in the case at hand it is a fact that (46) does hold.

It is immaterial, from this point of view, whether Move α is regarded as a rule forming S-structure from D-structure, or whether it is regarded as a property of S-structures that are "base-generated" (which now means: determined by X-bar theory, the Extended Projection Principle, and Case theory, with certain parameters fixed as indicated in earlier discussion). It is in fact far from clear that there is a distinction apart from terminology between these two formulations. (See Chomsky (1981a) and references cited there.)

Let us now return to the strong thesis of transformational generative grammar discussed earlier, namely, that the relation of GF-θ to GF-$\bar{\theta}$ is the same relation that holds between a *wh*-phrase or other operator (e.g. *O* of (43)) and its trace, between an extraposed phrase and the position in which it is interpreted, etc. Is this thesis correct? That is, do all of these relations satisfy the conditions (46a–c)? The answer resulting from the preceding discussion is that the thesis is indeed correct, as a matter of fact. The relation of GF-θ to GF-$\bar{\theta}$ has the properties of (46) and is therefore an instance of Move α, however the latter relation is construed: as a rule mapping D-structure to S-structure, or as a property of S-structure. The conditions (46a–c) also appear to hold of the other relations noted (see Chomsky (1981a) and references cited there; also note 20).

3. The Functional Determination of Empty Categories

Let us now examine the nature of the gaps we have been considering from a different and more general point of view. We have so far found three types of gap: PRO, NP-trace, and variable, the latter two being varieties of trace. An important property of these three types of EC is that they (virtually) partition the distribution of NP.[29] That is, the three types are in complementary distribution and among them (virtually) exhaust the possible NP positions. This property of ECs surely implies that there is only one type of EC and that the status of a particular occurrence of an EC as PRO, NP-trace, or variable is functionally determined, that is, determined by the EC's role in derivations and representations. The partitioning, which is otherwise mysterious, will then follow.

Assuming that this is the case, how do we determine the status of a particular gap? We can proceed as follows. To begin with, a category is a *variable* if it is in an A-position and is locally $\bar{A}$-bound. For example, *him* in (8b–d) is a variable, but trace in COMP or *he* in (47a) is not; rather, the latter is interpreted at LF essentially as it is in (47b), a fairly straightforward matter:

(47)
a. who$_i$ [t_i said that he$_i$ would win]
b. John$_i$ said that he$_i$ would win

In particular, an EC is a variable if it is in an A-position and is locally $\bar{\text{A}}$-bound. An EC in an A-position that is not a variable is an anaphor. Note that if not a variable, a pronoun is either free or locally A-bound by an antecedent with an independent θ-role. Extending this property to ECs, an EC that is not a variable is a pronominal if it is free or locally A-bound by an antecedent with an independent θ-role, again restricting ourselves to A-positions. PRO is, as required, a pronominal anaphor. Recall that it follows from the θ-Criterion and the Projection Principle that the antecedent of a trace t will always be in a position to which no independent θ-role is assigned: a $\bar{\theta}$-position which, furthermore, is not part of any chain other than the one formed by application of Move α to the position occupied by t. In this manner, we can determine for each EC its status as trace or PRO, and if trace, as an anaphor or R-expression (variable).

Let us now consider some consequences of this functional approach to the typology of ECs. Note first that an element may be moved by Move α leaving an EC which is PRO rather than a variable or pure anaphor; this possibility amounts to a rule substituting PRO for trace. In a pro-drop language, for example, if the matrix subject inverts and is adjoined to the VP, it leaves an EC that lacks a c-commanding antecedent and is therefore PRO, namely, the empty pleonastic element of (48) (which corresponds to English pleonastic *there* as in *there arrived three men)*:

(48)
PRO parla Giovanni
'Giovanni is speaking'

Another consequence has been pointed out by Dominique Sportiche. Consider again the strong crossover case (49) (= (18a)):

(49)
who does he think [t' [t likes Bill]]

Here t is the EC left by movement of *who,* and t' is the trace in COMP left by successive cyclic movement. The EC t is a variable since it is locally $\bar{\text{A}}$-bound. We have the option of taking the local $\bar{\text{A}}$-binder to be t' or the actual operator *who* in the COMP of the matrix sentence. In the latter case, we are in effect defining a variable as a category that is locally operator-bound, excluding the trace in COMP of an operator from the class of binders. This amounts to building principle (44) into the definition of the notion "variable". Taking this step has no effect apart from such cases as (49). Suppose that *he* and *t* are coindexed in (49). Then *t* is an EC locally A-bound by an element in a θ-position and is therefore PRO, by the functional definition. As PRO, however, it violates Principles A and B of the binding theory, since it is governed (namely, by the INFL element of the embedded clause (NIC)). Therefore, (49) is barred in the intended interpretation by Principles A and B of the binding theory; it is unnecessary to appeal to Principle C, as in the earlier discussion, since the basic content of this principle for variables has been built into the definition of the notion. This suggests that Principle C can be entirely eliminated, since strong crossover was in fact the most important reason for maintaining it. Other cases that fall under Principle C would then have to be dealt with in other ways.[30]

---

4. Parasitic Gaps

This functional approach to ECs, which is developed in more detail in chapter 6 of Chomsky (1981a), has a range of further empirical consequences of a rather interesting sort. Consider again the examples (10) and (11), which were given to illustrate the Koopman–Sportiche Bijection Principle:

(10)
his mother loves everyone   (in the sense: for each person x, x's mother loves x)

(11)
who did you give a picture of e to e

Example (10) illustrates the phenomenon of *weak crossover,* the designation *weak* being used (originally by Thomas Wasow) because the phenomenon is much less sharp than the "strong crossover" illustrated in (49). Similarly, judgments concerning such structures as (11) are often not sharp and vary among speakers, the structure being assigned a marginal status. This is a case of what Taraldsen (1979) and Engdahl (1981a) have called *parasitic gaps.*

The LF representations corresponding to (10) and (11) are (50a,b), respectively:

(50)

a. [everyone]$_i$ [his$_i$ mother loves e_i]

b. who$_i$ [did you give a picture of e_i to e_i]

In (50a), *he* (of *his*) and *e* are variables, each locally $\overline{\text{A}}$-bound by the operator *everyone*, violating the Bijection Principle, which strengthened the prohibition against vacuous operators to a one-to-one relation between operators and variables.[31] At LF, the Bijection Principle assigns to (50a) a marginal status as a "weak" violation. Similarly in (50b), each occurrence of *e* is a variable locally bound by *who*, again violating the Bijection Principle.

In Chomsky (1981a), I assumed that (50b) was ungrammatical, but that was not really correct; rather, it is more or less acceptable under the interpretation given, while other examples of a similar kind are quite acceptable, as we shall see directly. I pointed out that (11) (= (50b)) cannot be derived by Move α, since movement to either of the EC positions would violate the principle that only movement to a $\overline{\theta}$- position is allowed. On the assumption that each EC is either PRO or trace, there is no other possible derivation of (11).

Let us now reconsider (11) in the light of the functional interpretation of ECs. Suppose that its D-structure is either (51a) or (51b):

(51)

a. you INFL give a picture of *e* to who

b. you INFL give a picture of who to *e*

Suppose, for the sake of illustration, that the D-structure is (51a). Application of Move α gives the S-structure (52):

(52)

who did you give a picture of *e* to *t*

Here *t* is the trace of *who*, and is coindexed with *who*. Consider now the index of *e*. If it is distinct from the index of *who* and *t*, then *e* is by definition PRO and the structure is ungrammatical at S-structure by the binding theory, since *e* is governed PRO. The same holds if we derive (11) from (51b), with *e* of (51b) unbound. Therefore, this interpretation is impossible for (11).

Suppose, then, that the index of *e* is the same as that of *who* and its trace. Then *e* is a variable locally $\overline{\text{A}}$-bound by *who*. The binding theory is satisfied since *e* is A-free. Note that *e* in (51) is by definition PRO, but the fact that it is governed is of no significance since the binding theory applies only at S-structure and (51) is a D-structure. The θ-Criterion is satisfied at both D- and S-structure. In short, given the indexing in (50b), (11) is unproblematic with regard to the binding theory, the Projection Principle, the θ-Criterion, and the rule Move α. The Bijection Principle assigns (11) its marginal status at LF.

Suppose that in (51) we had selected an overt pronoun ultimately coindexed with *who* in place of *e*. The resulting forms are (53a,b):

(53)

a. who did you give a picture of him to *t*

b. who did you give a picture of *t* to him

Both examples violate weak crossover as determined by the Bijection Principle; note that the latter eliminates the left–right asymmetry in earlier versions of weak crossover such as Chomsky (1980b). There are further considerations bearing on *wh*-extraction and coindexing of *him* and *t*, which I will ignore here. Putting these aside, the two examples of (53) have the same status, approximately that of (50b).

Summarizing, the possibility of a parasitic gap interpretation, somewhat marginal in the light of the Bijection Principle, follows from the option of selecting a pronominal with or without phonological content at D-structure, in other words from the null hypothesis. To put it differently, the same optionality of choice of phonological content that permits the phenomenon of control and the existence of pro-drop languages with "missing subjects" provides for the existence of parasitic gaps such as (11). The existence of the phenomenon is therefore not surprising; it is exactly what we would expect, as is its somewhat marginal status. The same is true in such cases as (54a–c). (These and most of the subsequent examples are taken from Engdahl's important study (1981a), which contains references to earlier discussion.)

(54)

a. which articles did John file *t* without reading *e*

b. this is the kind of food you must cook *t* before you eat *e*

c. here is the influential professor that John sent his book to *t* in order to impress *e*

In each of these cases, *e* is a parasitic gap "licensed" by the real gap *t*, the trace of movement-to-COMP. The gap *e* is simply the phonologically null variant of the pronoun that may also appear in this position.

The parasitic gap is a variable at S-structure and at LF. We might say that it is syntactically a variable in that it falls within the scope of an operator, while it is semantically a pronominal as indicated by its D-structure status. Notice that if it proves to be appropriate to take this informal comment seriously, it amounts to assigning to the properties of D-structure a partially independent role in semantic interpretation, along the lines of earlier versions of EST. In section 5, we will suggest a slightly different and semantically more natural interpretation of the base-generated EC pronominal, relating it still more closely to the pronoun that can replace it in these constructions.

We noted earlier that properties of gaps are particularly interesting for several important reasons. While these also apply to parasitic gaps, the latter deserve our interest for other reasons as well. As noted, the phenomenon is a fairly marginal one. Nevertheless, speaker judgments often seem reasonably clear and consistent over a range of complex examples, as Engdahl shows and as will be further illustrated below; also, the basic properties are quite clear, though there are some interfering factors (perhaps having to do with processing difficulty, or with parallelism constraints and the like) that have to be set aside to discern them. Surely one would not expect that the parasitic gap phenomenon is sanctioned by special principles of UG or that there is a component of UG dealing specifically with the properties of these constructions. Furthermore, it is highly implausible to suppose that the basic properties are learned from exposure to examples identified as acceptable or unacceptable. Apart from the inherent implausibility, the marginal status of the construction rules out this assumption. What we expect, then, is that the properties of parasitic gap constructions, and the very existence of the phenomenon, will reduce to independently established principles of UG. This indeed seems to be the case, over quite an interesting range.

Parasitic gaps pose three major questions:

(55)

a. Why does the phenomenon exist at all?

b. What are the basic properties of parasitic gaps?

c. What principles and mechanisms determine these properties?

As noted, it is highly unlikely that new and independent principles need be invoked to answer these questions or that rules of particular grammar are involved.

We have already come upon a plausible answer for question (55a): the phenomenon arises from the null hypothesis, the optionality of phonological content for pronominals, the same property that accounts for control and the possibility of "missing subjects" in pro-drop languages. As for question (55b), the basic property of parasitic gaps is as stated in (56) (this is a first approximation, to be slightly refined later). (56) is essentially the formulation given by Taraldsen in the paper that both initiated the study of this topic and provided what I think to be basically the correct explanation for it (Taraldsen (1979)):

(56)
A parasitic gap is licensed by a variable that does not c-command it.

(56) is satisfied by the examples (50b) and (54a–c), which are typical in this respect. As for the status of (56), it follows from principles that we have already discussed and that are motivated on independent grounds, answering question (55c). Let us now clarify (56) and see why it follows from the principles of GB theory, following a line of argument rather close to that of Taraldsen (1979) but relying now on somewhat more general assumptions.[32]

Using Engdahl's terminology, we are concerned with structures of the form (57) (order irrelevant), where α is a *filler* and t is a *gap* associated with this filler by normal processes (that is, independently of the presence of e), while e is a gap that is not licensed independently of (α, t) (it is not the gap of some other filler):

(57)
...α...t...e...   (order irrelevant)

The gap t "licenses" e in the sense that it assigns α as the filler of e. In (54a), for example, the filler is *which articles* and its normal gap is t; the gap t licenses e by associating it with *which articles* as its filler.

Engdahl's formulation of (56) is (58):

(58)
A parasitic gap e is licensed by a gap t if
a. the relation of t to its filier is an unbounded dependency
b. t does not c-command e

We have replaced (58a) by the statement in (56) that α in (57) locally Ā-binds t. As we shall see, this reformulation is descriptively more adequate than (58a); much more importantly, though, it permits the descriptive statement that answers the question (55b) to be derived from independent principles. Engdahl notes that (58b) is "somewhat surprising" since "in this respect, the parasitic gap here behaves more like a lexical NP than like a pronoun." The property (58b), incorporated in (56), is no longer surprising in our terms: while e of (57) is a pronominal at D-structure and is in this sense semantically analogous to a phonetically realized pronoun, it is a variable $\bar{A}$-bound by α at S-structure; quite generally, variables behave in the manner of names with respect to the binding theory, as shown by strong crossover and inapplicability of Principles A and B of the binding theory (i.e. opacity violations).

Let us now seek to answer the question (55c). We want to show how (56) follows from the general principles that we have established on other grounds. First, we may adopt Engdahl's tacit assumption that e in (57) is in a governed A-position and heads a chain (possibly having e itself as its only member) that terminates in a θ-position and is assigned the corresponding θ-role. For if e is ungoverned, it is simply control PRO, irrelevant here (see also the later discussion of (83)); and the only possible case of e in an $\bar{A}$-position will be subject to the analysis of (40), hence again irrelevant. Suppose then that e is in a governed A-position heading a chain with no θ-role, where α c-commands e so as to overcome the binding theory violation of e. Suppose that α is an argument. Then it is assigned its θ-role independently of the chain headed by e, and since α c-commands e, e is PRO, which is impossible since it is governed. Therefore, α is a nonargument. For the same reason, if t c-commands e, then the chain including t cannot have a θ-role. There are few remaining possibilities, and their analysis is irrelevant. Note that e is in subject position (since there is no other $\bar{\theta}$-position that is an A-position) and that it must be properly governed, since it is trace, not PRO. The only possible example is one in which e is governed after S' Deletion by the verb of the clause containing (α, t), where t c-commands e; this gives an S-structure chain (α, t, e),[33] where α is a nonargument in an A-position (otherwise, t will be a variable, hence an R-expression requiring a θ-role). We may admit this case, or we may exclude it by whatever conditions prevent generation of raising constructions with nonargument heads without movement (e.g. the mechanisms of Chomsky (1981a), which require a "local" relation between a pleonastic element and the postposed phrase associated with it).

Suppose now that α is in an A-position in (57). Given that e is in a governed position heading a chain with an independent θ-role and is c-commanded by α, it follows that α is an argument assigned a θ-role by the chain headed by e. Then the D-structure position of α (namely, the position of t) must be a θ-position. But then e is PRO, since its antecedent has an independent θ-role, violating the binding theory since it is governed. Furthermore, even if we were to drop this functional characterization of ECs, the structure (57) is barred by the θ-Criterion: if t c-commands e, then α heads the chain (α, t, e), violating the θ-Criterion since the chain is assigned a dual θ-role; and if t does not c-command e, then α heads the two chains (α, t), (α, e), again violating the θ-Criterion since α is assigned a dual θ-role. Note crucially that this conclusion does not follow if α is in COMP, since an $\bar{A}$-binder in COMP does not head a chain; it is not an argument that receives a θ-role from the position of its trace.

It follows that e in (57) cannot be assigned the status of NP-trace A-bound by α in S-structure to overcome the binding theory violation. In other words, the parasitic gap cannot be licensed by an NP-trace t. Therefore, t is $\bar{A}$-bound by α and is thus a variable with a θ-role. If t c-commands e, we have a case already excluded. Therefore, as stated in (56), α is in an $\bar{A}$-position and t does not c-command e.

In summary, the answers to questions (55a–c) are as follows: (a) the parasitic gap phenomenon exists because phonological features are optional for pronominals, as shown by control and pro-drop languages; (b) the basic properties of parasitic gaps are as stated in (56); (c) this follows from the binding theory, the θ-Criterion, and the Projection Principle (and, independently, the functional characterization of ECs), all of which enter into the foregoing discussion.

This analysis accounts for a large variety of improper choices of parasitic gaps, including those that Engdahl discusses. For example:

(59)

a. John was called t an idiot as often as Mary called $\left\{ \begin{array}{l} \text{him} \\ \text{*PRO} \end{array} \right\}$ a cretin

b. John was killed t by a tree falling on $\left\{ \begin{array}{l} \text{him} \\ \text{*PRO} \end{array} \right\}$

c. John seems [t to have met $\left\{ \begin{array}{l} \text{*him} \\ \text{*PRO} \end{array} \right\}$]

d. John seems [t to have (been) read [my story about $\begin{Bmatrix} him \\ *PRO \end{Bmatrix}$]]

e. who [t (was) sent a picture of $\begin{Bmatrix} *him \\ *PRO \end{Bmatrix}$]

f. who [t expected [Bill to send a picture of $\begin{Bmatrix} him \\ *PRO \end{Bmatrix}$]]

g. who did you present $\begin{Bmatrix} *him \\ *PRO \end{Bmatrix}$ to t

Throughout, we are concerned only with *him* coindexed with *John* or the trace of *who*.

In each example of (59), exactly as in (52)–(54), we may select either *him* or PRO at D-structure in the position indicated. Choice of *him* is subject to Principle B of the binding theory. Choice of PRO is ruled out by the considerations just discussed in all of these examples. Example (59g) illustrates the fact (pointed out by Youssef Aoun) that both (56) and (58) are descriptively inadequate, in that in this case the parasitic gap c-commands the trace of movement rather than conversely, but the construction is still excluded. Choice of *him* is excluded as a strong crossover violation. Choice of PRO is barred for the same reasons under our assumptions (Taraldsen's formulation of (56) correctly excluded (59g) by the requirement that the parasitic gap not c-command the real gap). Note that the descriptive statement (56) has no status in the grammar, simply being a consequence of principles of UG. We will see later that this descriptive statement must be still further modified, again, a fact without significance in our terms.

Compare (59a) with (60):

(60)

a. a man who Mary called t an idiot as often as Jane called $\begin{Bmatrix} him \\ PRO \end{Bmatrix}$ a cretin

b. who did Mary call t an idiot as often as Jane called $\begin{Bmatrix} him \\ PRO \end{Bmatrix}$ a cretin

Here, either PRO or *him* yields a well-formed S-structure, contrasting with (59a). Choice of PRO in (60) yields a variable $\bar{A}$-bound by *who*, while in (59a) it yields a pronominal A-bound by *John*. Therefore, (59a) is a "strong" violation of fundamental principles (those invoked in the preceding analysis), while (60) is only a "weak" violation of the Bijection Principle at LF, which explains the acceptability ranking. Unaccounted for here is a clear preference for *him* over PRO in (60).

Pursuing the matter further, Engdahl cites some experimental evidence that in (61) there is a slight preference for PRO—i.e. the parasitic gap—over the overt pronoun:

(61)

here is the student that my attempt to talk to $\left\{ \begin{array}{l} \text{him} \\ \text{PRO} \end{array} \right\}$ scared *t* to death

Both choices violate the Bijection Principle at LF; the pronoun case is an instance of weak crossover. If the two possibilities in fact differ in status, this might indicate that the Bijection Principle applies "more strongly" in this case to overt pronouns at LF than to gaps. Comparison with the opposite ranking in (60) might indicate that some left–right asymmetry, or perhaps a distinction between gaps in tensed clauses and in nominals, is involved. As Engdahl notes, the example (61) is in a sense complementary to the normal use of the resumptive pronoun strategy, seen in (8c,d), to overcome island violations. In that case, a pronoun interpreted as a variable is used to overcome conditions that preclude a gap; in the case of (61), a gap is slightly preferred to overcome the weak crossover constraint that (weakly) bars an overt pronoun. While the facts are not very sharp, the conclusion seems not implausible, and warrants further study. However, see note 11 and the discussion of (101) later in this section.

Examples (62a,b) support the conclusion that the binding theory applies at S-structure:

(62)

a. I forget who filed every article without reading $\left\{ \begin{array}{l} \text{it} \\ \text{*PRO} \end{array} \right\}$

b. I forget who filed which article without reading $\left\{ \begin{array}{l} \text{it} \\ \text{*PRO} \end{array} \right\}$

We interpret (62b) as a multiple *wh*-construction rather than an echo question. At S-structure the EC object of *reading* is free in the intended interpretation and is therefore ruled out as governed PRO. At LF, however, the EC is $\overline{\text{A}}$-bound by the quantifier or *wh*-phrase moved to an

A̅-position by a rule of the LF component, so that if the binding theory were to apply only at LF, the sentence should be acceptable as a parasitic gap.

Notice further that parasitic gaps provide additional evidence for a movement-to-COMP analysis of complex adjectival constructions along the lines discussed in Chomsky (1977) and elsewhere. We have already found strong evidence to support this conclusion in connection with (63) (= (40)):

(63)
the men are too stubborn to talk to (Bill)

Now consider the analogous structure (64), where (b) is the S-structure following the assumptions of Chomsky (1977) (here somewhat simplified, with the operator taken to be vacuous rather than a *wh*-phrase subsequently deleted):

(64)
a. this book is too interesting to put down without having finished
b. this book is too interesting [*O* [PRO to put *t* down without PRO having finished *e*]]

The structure (64b) is an instance of (57) with $\alpha = O$; that is, *t* is the trace of the empty operator *O* moved to COMP in the syntax, and *e* is the parasitic gap licensed by the variable *t*. If there were no such operator *O*, the structure would be barred for reasons already discussed: *e* would be an NP-trace A-bound by *this book* (structurally analogous to (59b), in which α locally A-binds *t* and *e*), rather than being assigned the status of a parasitic gap, as it is. We may say that there is a "filler– gap" relation between *this book* and *t* in (64), but it is established only indirectly, in the manner discussed in connection with (63) (= (40)).

Engdahl takes (64a) to show that parasitic gaps can occur in constructions without movement, contrary to the proposal of Chomsky and Lasnik (1977) that we have now recast in the GB framework.[34] However, she does not consider the possibility of an analysis along the lines of Chomsky (1977), which I believe to be quite well motivated for reasons discussed there and elsewhere (for example, in connection with (63) (= (40)) or the purposive constructions discussed in Chomsky (1980a,b)). We can thus reverse her argument and take (64) to provide still more evidence that there is indeed movement in these cases.

Compare (64) with (65):

(65)

a. the books were put down (sold, . . .) without having finished (them)
b. the books were sold at a low price to help students
c. the books sold at a low price to help students
d. the books can be sold without reading (them)

In contrast to (64), (65a) is impossible with a parasitic gap or a pronominal object in the *without*-phrase. This is because the PRO subject of the latter phrase cannot be arbitrary in interpretation for some reason, but must be controlled. (Redundantly, the parasitic gap is excluded since it is A-bound by *the books* rather than $\overline{\text{A}}$-bound by O, as in (64).) In (64), this PRO subject is controlled by the PRO subject of the embedded clause of the complex adjectival construction; but there is no controller in (65a), so that the construction is ungrammatical. This contrast provides further evidence for the Extended Projection Principle, which requires the presence of the PRO subject of the embedded clause in (64b).

Note that in other constructions, the "understood subject" of the missing *by*-phrase can serve as a kind of controller, as we see in (65b) as compared with the much less acceptable (65c); see Chomsky (1981a) (citing observations of Rita Manzini) and Marantz (1981). Note also that the requirement that the subject of the gerund be controlled rather than arbitrary involves other factors, which are poorly understood. Thus, consider (65d), which is acceptable with a pronoun object in the *without*-clause (the parasitic gap is again excluded because it would be A-bound).

As Engdahl observes, the parasitic gap phenomenon often provides evidence about constituent structure. For example, neither the *before*-clause of (54b) nor the *without*-phrase of (64) is in the c-command domain of the verb of its clause, or the parasitic gap e will be c-commanded by the gap t that licenses it. Such evidence is not provided by the fact that a pronoun can appear in the position of the parasitic gap coindexed with the licensing trace, since such a pronoun is in any event free in its governing category (SSC). These observations bear not only on constituent structure, but also perhaps on the proper formulation of the notion of c-command, a matter discussed but left unresolved in note 14. To see why, consider what the constituent structure must be for the phrase containing the parasitic gap (call it E) to fail to be c-commanded by the verb V as required. Plainly, E cannot be a sister to V. Therefore, it is either (I) an immediate constituent of S, or (II) an immediate constituent of VP* containing E and VP as its two constituents, where VP is the phrase consisting of V and its complements—thus a construction having the form (i) of note 14, repeated here:

(66)

$[_{VP*}[_{VP} V...] \alpha]$

Here $\alpha = E$. Consider (I). If INFL is the head of S, as we have assumed, then E is not c-commanded by V, as required. If V is the head of S, then we cannot adopt the extended sense of c-command discussed in connection with (34). Consider (II). Since V is the head of VP* in (66), we cannot adopt the extended sense of c-command. Assuming this extended sense to be accurate, then (66) is ruled out for these constructions, and (I) must hold with INFL the head of S. Alternatively, we may adopt the extended notion of c-command only for heads, not their complements.

Engdahl notes further that parasitic gaps may be triggered by Heavy NP Shift, as in (67):

(67)

John offended t by not recognizing e immediately, his favorite uncle from Cleveland

Here t is the trace of the rightward-moved NP and e is the parasitic gap; in terms of (57), $\alpha = $ *his favorite uncle from Cleveland*. If the moved NP had been left in place, the gap would not be permitted, since e would be governed PRO. (Note that t does not c-command e, but *him* is possible in place of e without disjoint reference in any event by Principle B of the binding theory (SSC).)

Example (67) follows from the principles of GB theory on the assumption that the rightward movement is to an $\overline{A}$-position in (67), an assumption that we would adopt independently of these considerations since there is no GF associated with this position. Then t and e are $\overline{A}$-bound in (67), Case-marked as we would expect for R-expressions. Technically, t and e are variables in the sense of this term introduced earlier. (The terminology, however, is no longer felicitous; we might preferably restrict the term *variable* to the subclass of $\overline{A}$-bound categories that are operator-bound, or perhaps even more narrowly.) Hence, the example falls within the present framework.

Recall that Engdahl formulated the descriptive principle (58) rather than our (56) to characterize parasitic gaps. The difference is that in (56) the licensing gap is required to be $\overline{A}$-bound, while in (58) it is required to be related to its filler by an unbounded dependency. The formulation in (56) is preferable because it permits us to derive the properties of parasitic gaps from independent principles rather than stipulating them specifically for the parasitic gap phenomenon, always a desideratum and particularly so in the present case for reasons already discussed. But (67) shows that (56) is also descriptively preferable to (58). Such examples as (67) are inconsistent with (58a) unless we assume Heavy NP Shift to be a rule that gives rise to unbounded rightward dependencies, thus in the same class with result clause interpretation and comparatives that tolerate split antecedents rather than with such rules as relative clause extraposition (see Chomsky (1981a, chapter 2)). However, this assumption is untenable.

The concept "unbounded dependency" is, furthermore, a very dubious one. Thus, consider (68):

(68)
a. who$_i$ does John seem [to be certain [to like e_i]]
b. John$_i$ seems [to be certain [to be liked e_i]]
c. John$_i$ seems [to be too stubborn [to like e_i]]

We may understand the use of e and coindexing to be a theory-neutral representation of the relationship that exists between the antecedent and the object of *like,* whatever mechanisms are assumed (in our terms, successive cyclic movement in (68a) and (68b) and the mechanisms discussed in connection with (40) in (68c)). The relation of *who* to e in (68a) is held to be an "unbounded dependency", while in contrast the structurally parallel relation of *John* to e in (68b) is a "bounded dependency"; (68c) is then described as a "mixed case", involving an unbounded dependency between e and the subject of *too stubborn . . .* and a bounded dependency between *John* and this subject. These are highly theory-internal characterizations. It seems to me merely a stipulation to place the constructions into these various categories, and one that is quite unwarranted. As we have seen, all three cases fall under Move α (= (46)) in their basic properties, with (68c) now recast in the manner motivated in the discussion of (40) and (64). Furthermore, the evidence for successive cyclic movement (i.e. reduction to bounded dependency) is considerably stronger for constructions such as (68a) and the complex adjectival construction of (68c) than it is for (68b) or the "raising" subpart of (68c). On the former, see the references of note 20. On the latter, I know of no comparable argument. In fact, some form of boundedness corresponding to our successive cyclicity is built into the treatment of the former construction even in some of the approaches that treat them as "unbounded dependencies", e.g. Bresnan and Grimshaw (1978). Therefore, if one wished to adhere to the terminology, it would be more reasonable to invert it, referring to (68a) and the internal part of (68c) as a "bounded dependency", and to (68b) and the external part of (68c) as perhaps an "unbounded dependency". In fact, however, there is no reason to introduce the notions "bounded" and "unbounded" at all in connection with (68).

There are, indeed, constructions that are not subject to the constraints of bounding theory and may in this sense be described as "unbounded": for example, result clause interpretation, certain types of comparatives, association of antecedents with overt anaphors, control (see the discussion of (23), (35)), multiple wh-constructions (i.e. LF movement), and the A-binding found in such examples as (40). But (68) does not fall within this category. The processes that may properly be described as "unbounded" involve "interpretation to the left" (for instance, the first two cases listed above) or "interpretation to the right". In these cases there is independent evidence that no movement is involved in the syntax, so that it seems correct to assume, as we have done, that the theory of bounding is part of the theory of syntactic (not LF) movement.

The crucial distinction between (68a) and (68b) is, I believe, exactly what it appears to be on the surface: a distinction between $\overline{\text{A}}$-binding and A-binding, one that is central to binding and θ-theory and that carries over directly to the theory of parasitic gaps. This distinction is simply a descriptive fact, common to all theories. As we have seen, there is strong reason to assimilate the internal part of (68c) to (68a), with $\overline{\text{A}}$-binding; see the references cited for independent support for this conclusion. There is in fact a principled distinction between (68a) and the internal part of (68c) on the one hand, and (68b) and the external part of (68c) on the other: namely, the same rule of Move α (= (46)) yields $\overline{\text{A}}$-binding in the first case and A-binding in the second. But the distinction between A-binding and $\overline{\text{A}}$-binding, a descriptive fact common to all theories, suffices to account for all of the relevant properties of (68) without introducing any further (and highly dubious) distinction

between "bounded" and "unbounded" dependencies in these cases—
though, as noted, there is good reason to distinguish the processes involved in (68) from others that are indeed "unbounded" and that for
independent reasons clearly do not involve Move α.

Engdahl argues that "the parasitic gap facts provide an argument
against subsuming *wh*-type movement and NP-type movement under
one and the same rule and for making a systematic distinction in the
grammar between bounded and unbounded processes." This conclusion seems to me incorrect, in both respects. The parasitic gap facts
suggest no distinction between the two types of movement rule apart
from the uncontroversial distinction between $\overline{\text{A}}$- and A-binding (note
that the distinction is not obvious, but is well justified, in the case of
(68c)). If we reduce both types of movement to Move α and do not
introduce a distinction (which seems quite artificial) between bounded
and unbounded processes in these cases, then we can reduce the parasitic gap phenomenon to the general optionality of phonological content for pronominals, explaining the basic facts in terms of independent
and quite plausible principles. These are the conceptually preferable
assumptions, and they seem well supported by the facts.

Even if a distinction could be established between bounded and unbounded processes in the manner often assumed in the case of (68), and
even if there were no counterevidence such as Heavy NP Shift to the
assumption that parasitic gaps are associated with unbounded processes, the latter association would not constitute an explanation, but
rather a fact to be explained (thus, why should parasitic gaps not be
associated solely with bounded processes, or with some other property?). In contrast, we hope to establish, for the reasons already discussed, that the properties of the parasitic gap constructions simply
follow from independently established principles, given structural information about sentences that is independently grounded. It is this
approach that Taraldsen followed, along lines that we have slightly re-
vised, in the paper that opened this topic to investigation, and surely he
was right to do so.

Other properties of parasitic gaps also support the conclusion that
there is no relevant distinction in terms of boundedness but only in
terms of A-binding versus $\overline{\text{A}}$-binding. Engdahl observes that parasitic
gaps are commonly found in positions that block extraction and in fact
notes "that a parasitic gap does not survive easily as an independent

gap"; that is, parasitic gaps tend to appear in positions that resist extraction. In (69), for example, the parasitic gap e is in a position that is relatively inaccessible to movement:

(69)

a. here is the influential professor that John sent his book to t in order to impress e (= (54c))

b. this is the type of book that no one who has read e would give t to his mother

c. he is a man whom everyone who meets e admires t

d. whom did your interest in e surprise t

As we can see by replacing t, e by lexical NPs, the position represented by e is indeed the parasitic gap and is relatively inaccessible to movement (a fact to which I will return).[35] Why should parasitic gaps occur in positions that do not readily tolerate *wh*-movement? This would be particularly surprising if the conditions that constrain the movement phenomenon (however it is construed) are held to be associated with unbounded dependency. The relation of the filler to the parasitic gap is no less "unbounded" than that of the filler to the real gap; if unboundedness were the property correlated with island phenomena, then there would be no reason for these conditions to be relaxed in the case of parasitic gaps. Engdahl makes the plausible observation that the appearance of parasitic gaps in domains relatively (as we shall see later, absolutely) inaccessible to ordinary extraction raises serious doubts about functional explanations for island phenomena in terms of parsing strategies and the like, since it is hard to see why these strategies should be suspended in the case of parasitic gaps. On our assumptions, exactly this property of parasitic gaps is expected. Since e is base-generated as an EC pronominal and is not subject to Move α, it is not subject to the island constraints that follow from bounding theory. Taraldsen (1979) observes further that such examples as (69c) (he gives similar examples and their Norwegian counterparts) support the conclusion that Subjacency (or whatever principles one assumes to be involved in the island phenomena) is a condition on movement rules rather than on representations, since on the latter assumption it would again be unclear why Subjacency should be relaxed in the case of the parasitic gap.

Furthermore, the reason why parasitic gaps in fact tend to occur in positions that are relatively inaccessible to movement becomes clear when we consider the kinds of structures that can be analyzed as cases of (57): for example, prepositional phrases that are not governed by V, purpose clauses, and the like.

Summarizing, it seems implausible to seek a distinction in (68) in terms of some sort of boundedness of dependency, or to suppose that there is any relevant distinction other than those that follow from the nature of the binding: Ā-binding or A-binding. Clearly this distinction is present, uncontroversially in the case of (68a) versus (68b) and through a more complex but I think persuasive course of argument in the case of (68b) versus the internal part of (68c). The null hypothesis, then, is that the binding distinction is the only relevant distinction. There seems to be every reason to accept this result, along with the further conclusion that there is no distinction of "boundedness" between (68a) and (68b).

Note again the analogue to a familiar observation about the resumptive pronoun strategy: namely, that it is generally immune to conditions following from bounding theory, as we would expect, since it does not involve Move α. Analogously, in the present case a gap is immune to these conditions. In both instances, the reason is the same: the element—in one case a pronoun, in the other case PRO—is base-generated rather than formed by movement. Thus, the possibility of such apparent "island violations" is not associated with the presence of overt phonological features, as consideration of just the resumptive pronoun strategy might suggest, but rather with application of Move α.

The situation is more complex, however. Engdahl notes that there are conditions of a still rather unclear nature that lead to a hierarchy of acceptability for parasitic gaps, as is evident from some of the examples cited above. Some of these conditions (e.g. finiteness of the clause containing the gap) appear to be similar to conditions that render complex adjectival constructions and others such as (68c), (64) relatively unacceptable (see Chomsky (1977; 1981a), Rizzi (1980a), Engdahl (1981b)). However, a look at further examples suggests that more is involved. Consider for instance (70):

(70)
a. he is a man whom everyone who meets the woman who marries *e* admires *t*
b. these are the articles that Bill wrote *t* without [PRO correcting *e*]
c. these are the articles that you knew [Bill wrote *t*] even without [PRO analyzing *e*]

d. these are the articles that you knew [*t* were written by Bill] even
without [PRO analyzing *e*]

In case (70a), the parasitic gap is in a more deeply embedded position
than in (69c), and the construction is less acceptable. While (70b) is an
acceptable parasitic gap construction with PRO controlled by *Bill*,
(70c) with PRO controlled by *you* is much less so, though the parasitic
gap is in a comparable position in the two cases. In (70d), with PRO
controlled by *you* and the gap again in a comparable position, the construction is completely unacceptable. It may be that (70d) is ruled out
by Case conflict: the relative operator inherits nominative Case from *t*,
but *e* has objective Case. It is possible that the other examples reflect a
parallelism constraint of a more general kind; but whatever additional
factors may be involved in many such cases as these, it is most unlikely, for reasons already discussed, that these factors are specific to
parasitic gap constructions.

Consider next such examples as (71a–c):

(71)
a. someone who John expected *t* would be successful though believing
e is incompetent.
b. this is the student everyone thinks *t* is intelligent because John said *e*
was intelligent
c. a woman who *t* called John an idiot as often as *e* called him a cretin

In these cases a parasitic gap is impossible in the position of *e*, which
must be filled by a pronoun. Taraldsen has suggested that such examples violate the ECP. This approach is contrary to the analysis of such
examples as (71b) and (60) (first discussed by Joan Bresnan) in Chomsky and Lasnik (1977).

The ECP approach seems correct, though it does not appear to tell
the whole story. Note that this analysis comes close to eliminating the
possibility of a parasitic gap in subject position. If what superficially
appears to be a parasitic gap in subject position is ungoverned, it is
interpreted as PRO; see the discussion of (83) later in this section. By
the ECP, a parasitic gap is excluded from the position of subject of a
finite clause. Thus, *e* lacks a proper governor in (71) though *t* has one
throughout, namely, the trace in COMP in (71a,b) and *who* in COMP in
(71c). The only possible subject parasitic gap, then, will be in an Excep-

tional Case-marking construction. Compare (71a–c) with the corresponding examples (72a–c):

(72)

a. someone who John expected *t* to be successful though believing *e* to be incompetent
b. this is the student everyone expected *t* to be intelligent because John believed *e* to be intelligent
c. a man who Mary called *t* an idiot as often as Jane called *e* a cretin (= (60a))
d. this is the student everyone expected you would like *t* because John said he liked *e*

In (72a–c), as contrasted with the corresponding examples (71a–c), the parasitic gap *e* is properly governed by the preceding verb so that there is no ECP violation. Examples (72a) and (72c) seem more acceptable than the corresponding ECP violations (71a) and (71c), as expected; example (72b), however, seems unacceptable. It may be that other factors such as those already mentioned are involved here, since (72d) also seems unacceptable though there is again no ECP violation. In general, there is plainly much more to learn about the factors that enter into determining the status of parasitic gap constructions beyond those that follow directly from the previously discussed principles of GB theory, though the latter do appear to account for a substantial core of significant cases.

Suppose that the ECP is, as just proposed, at least one factor in barring (71a–c). Note that in these cases the complementizer *that* does not appear before the parasitic gap *e*. While the ECP subsumes the *[*That*-Trace] Filter of Chomsky and Lasnik (1977), it is more general in that it also applies when the complementizer is missing, as long as there is no properly governing element in COMP. The examples of (71) support this generalization of the filter, as do examples of other kinds discussed in Chomsky (1981a, chapter 4), based largely on work by Richard Kayne, though in general the judgments in the relevant (and somewhat exotic) cases are not as clear as one would like. It seems, then, that the assumption that the ungrammatical status of such sentences as *who did you think that* t *left* reflects the presence of a complementizer or properties of movement or other such particularities was incorrect, a result of considering too narrow a range of examples.

Nevertheless, unresolved questions remain. Thus, examples (71a,b) become much worse if *that* appears before the parasitic gap *e*.

David Pesetsky observes that parasitic gaps are impossible if a PP is moved to COMP and the parasitic gap is an NP, as in (73a,b):

(73)
a. a book from which I copied *t* without buying *e*
b. a book that I copied from *t* without buying *e*

Case (73b) is acceptable, but (73a) is not. It is reasonable to assume that at LF, both examples have a representation something like (74):

(74)
a book [*O* [I copied from *t*] without buying *e*]

The structure (74) is one that should license parasitic gaps. If in fact (74) is (in the relevant respects) the common LF representation of (73a,b), this again supports the conclusion that binding theory applies at S-structure, since it is binding theory that must crucially distinguish between these cases if our earlier discussion is correct, and since it is at S-structure that the two cases differ in the relevant respects.

Still assuming (74) to be in essence the common LF representation of (73a,b), these examples provide an argument in favor of deriving (74) by a reconstruction rule of the LF component rather than by dissociating movement into copying and deletion, so that the S-structure of (73a) would be something like (75):

(75)
a book [from which [I copied [from which] without buying *e*]]

If the latter approach were correct, leaving what has sometimes been called a "layered trace", then the two cases of (73) should not differ in the relevant respects at S-structure. In general, the kinds of phenomena adduced in support of a copying-plus-deletion analysis of movement are found even in cases where a movement analysis is impossible, as in (76), strongly suggesting that this is not the right approach to these questions and that some sort of reconstruction rule is necessary:

(76)
PRO to be 18 years old is what every child wants most

For further discussion of this still rather murky topic, see Burzio (1981), Chomsky (1981a), and references cited there.

This discussion has been based on the underlying assumption that particular grammars should not have specific rules governing parasitic gaps and moreover that UG should not include specific principles governing this phenomenon. This appears to be a plausible assumption, for reasons already mentioned, and I believe that the preceding discussion lends it considerable support. It follows, then, that if languages appear to differ in the distribution of parasitic gaps, the difference should be reducible to independent properties of these languages. This is an extremely strong claim. If we assume it to be true, as seems plausible both on general grounds and in terms of the analysis so far discussed, then the study of parasitic gaps should prove quite useful for the investigation of typological and structural differences, since any differences among languages would have to be traceable somehow to independent properties of these languages. Engdahl has made some interesting remarks on this topic with regard to English and Swedish. Another possible case is noted by Donca Steriade. As we have seen, complex adjectival constructions involving internal movement-to-COMP permit parasitic gaps in English. Correspondingly, we expect to find, and do find, parasitic gaps in such constructions as (77a), alongside the "long-distance" movement-to-COMP illustrated in (77b):

(77)
a. the book is hard to buy *t* without reading *e*
b. the book is hard to convince people to buy *t* (that they should buy *t*)

However, the examples corresponding to (77a) seem less acceptable in the Romance languages, and constructions such as (77b) are also unacceptable. It may be, then, that the internal movement-to-COMP analysis that is well motivated for English constructions of this type is wrong for the Romance languages, so that *t* in the analogue to (77a) is not an $\bar{\text{A}}$-bound EC and therefore does not license a parasitic gap for reasons already discussed. If this line of reasoning (which has many consequences that I will not pursue) proves to be correct, it would provide an additional argument in favor of the movement-to-COMP analysis of complex adjectival constructions in English.

Consider the examples (78a–d):

(78)
a. Mary is pretty to look at *t*
b. Mary is pretty to look at *t* even without meeting *e*

c. Mary is pretty to tell people to look at *t*
d. it is pretty to look at Mary

Examples (78c) and (78d) are impossible, suggesting that there is no movement-to-COMP in these cases, though it is not clear then what the analysis should be. If there is no movement-to-COMP, we would expect not to find a parasitic gap in such cases as (78b). While the example seems to me more marginal than many other parasitic gap cases, it is surely far more acceptable than, say, the examples of (59) (for example, (59b), which should be structurally comparable to (78b) if the EC object of *look at* is an NP-trace here). This suggests that there is indeed internal movement-to-COMP even in such cases as (78a), though the matrix subject is evidently a θ-position, as distinct from (77). The impossibility of (78c) would then have to be explained on other grounds.

There are further ramifications. Consider the reanalysis approach to the constructions of (77) discussed in Chomsky (1981a, chapter 5). If that analysis is correct, then *t* is in effect an NP-trace in (77). However, (77a) indicates that it still retains its status as an A̅-bound trace at S-structure. The reanalysis approach requires that reanalysis occur in the syntax, prior to S-structure; otherwise, there will be a θ-Criterion violation at S-structure. Thus, we cannot account for these facts by assuming reanalysis to be a rule of the LF component. We are led, then, to an interpretation of reanalysis that assumes both the reanalyzed and the nonreanalyzed structures to be available at S-structure. This is entirely feasible, if we regard phrase markers as sets of strings rather than tree-like structures; see Chomsky (1955; 1981a), and Lasnik and Kupin (1977), and section 1 of this study. The implications seem worth pursuing, but I will not do so here.

There are many other related questions. To cite one, we have so far been considering parasitic gaps licensed by normal gaps created by movement-to-COMP. A natural question is whether resumptive pronouns can license parasitic gaps. English is not the best case to study in this regard since the resumptive pronoun strategy is marginal. However, consider such cases as (79a–d):

(79)
a. a man whom everyone who meets *e* knows someone who likes *e*
b. a man whom everyone who meets him knows someone who likes *e*
c. a man whom everyone who meets *e* knows someone who likes him
d. a man whom to know *e* is to like *e*

In case (79a), whichever occurrence of *e* is regarded as the parasitic gap, the other gap is inaccessible to movement. We therefore expect replacement of both gaps by *him* under the resumptive pronoun strategy generally adopted in such cases, and this yields an acceptable instance of the use of resumptive pronouns. In (79b,c), *him* is the resumptive pronoun normally used in such island violations (compare (8c)). Nevertheless, neither (79b) nor (79c) is acceptable. The same holds under the various replacements of *e* by *him* in (79d): replacing neither occurrence or both occurrences of *e* by *him* is preferable to replacing only one occurrence. These facts indicate that a resumptive pronoun cannot license a parasitic gap.

It would be reasonable to investigate this question in languages that use the resumptive pronoun strategy more freely than standard English does. Noting the following examples, Esther Torrego points out that appositive relatives allow resumptive pronouns quite freely in Spanish:

(80)

a. el reloj de que me hablaste, el cual han conseguido arreglar *t* [sin mover *e*], ha quedado muy bien

b. el reloj de que me hablaste, que *lo* han conseguido arreglar [sin mover *e*], ha quedado muy bien
    'the clock you spoke to me about, which they got to fix (*it*) [without moving], now works very well'

Example (80a) is grammatical but (80b) is not, though it becomes grammatical if the bracketed phrase is deleted, indicating that the italicized resumptive pronoun *lo* is permitted in this construction. The only difference between (80a) and (80b) is that (80b) has a resumptive pronoun in the position of the gap that licenses a parasitic gap in (80a). Again, it appears that a resumptive pronoun cannot license a parasitic gap.

Before we examine why this should be so, consider the case of a pro-drop language employing the resumptive pronoun strategy, so that the "missing subject" can serve as a resumptive pronoun (see Taraldsen (1978b) for discussion of such a case in one variety of Italian, reviewed briefly in Chomsky (1981a, chapter 4)). Does such a subject license a parasitic gap? The question is interesting, since the "missing" resumptive pronoun subject is indistinguishable in its feature content from a variable left by *Wh* Movement. It is not clear whether relevant examples can be constructed because of the structural requirements that must be satisfied. I will proceed on the tentative assumption that even in this case a resumptive pronoun cannot license a parasitic gap, despite the fact that it is indistinguishable in intrinsic content from a variable that can do so. The reason will appear directly.

So far, I have been restricting attention to structures of the form (57), in which a parasitic gap is licensed by a normal gap. But so far nothing in this discussion prevents base-generation of PRO in place of a pronoun in any position, associated with a base-generated *wh*-phrase (or other operator) in COMP position and interpreted as the variable bound by this phrase, as in (81):

(81)
wh- [...*e*...]

Clearly this possibility must be excluded; otherwise, we would be able to form constructions freely violating island conditions, in effect treating base-generated PRO as a resumptive pronoun. This problem is not specifically related to the parasitic gap phenomenon; it concerns the proper way of dealing with the resumptive pronoun strategy. We cannot exclude the possibility of generating the *wh*-phrase in the COMP position, since this is required in some cases when the resumptive pronoun strategy is employed. Nor can we exclude the possibility of taking an EC to be a resumptive pronominal, since this is just what we find where an EC appears as a "missing subject" in a pro-drop language. It must be, then, that *e* in (81) is not a variable but a pronominal at S-structure, where the binding theory applies. Therefore, *e* is not locally Ā-bound at S-structure. That is, the *wh*-phrase or other operator base-generated in COMP must lack an index at S-structure.

The natural general principle that will subsume this case is that the free indexing procedure at S-structure is restricted to A-positions. Thus, *wh-* in (81) has no index at S-structure. But *wh*-phrases base-generated in COMP do have indices at LF, as in the case of the resumptive pronoun strategy, where such a phrase binds a variable that may be a pronoun or an EC. Therefore, there must be an indexing procedure for Ā-positions (though not A-positions) in the LF component.

Summarizing, then, we assume that A-positions are indexed at S-structure and Ā-positions at LF, though an element in an Ā-position may have an index at S-structure if it is moved to this position in the syntax.

Let us now consider resumptive pronouns a bit more closely, recalling some earlier remarks. The discussion so far has left open the question of whether there is a base-generated operator in the case of relative clause constructions with a resumptive pronoun. Suppose that there is. Then either this operator must be coindexed with the resumptive pronoun at LF or the construction is excluded by the barrier against vacuous operators. Languages differ, then, according to whether or not they allow such indexing of an $\bar{A}$-position at LF. A language lacking the resumptive pronoun strategy rejects this option, while one admitting this strategy accepts it. In both kinds of language, the EC resumptive pronominal will appear only in a position in which an EC pronominal is permissible at S-structure, as determined by the pro-drop parameter: essentially, the subject of a finite clause. At LF, the EC is a variable, one that may violate island conditions in a language employing the resumptive pronoun strategy. Since e in (81) is a pronominal rather than a variable at S-structure, the construction is barred in a non-pro-drop language (but see below for further complications). It also follows that resumptive elements cannot license parasitic gaps, whether they are phonetically realized as in (79) or phonetically empty as in a pro-drop language, even though in the latter case, the resumptive EC is indistinguishable from a variable that can license a parasitic gap. It also follows that the principle involved in the pro-drop parameter applies at S-structure.

Let us now consider the other alternative. Suppose that there is no operator base-generated in COMP in clauses with a resumptive pronoun (so that, as noted earlier, the overt operator in such constructions as (8b,c) or (79) would have to be regarded as somehow an analogic form). Suppose, in particular, that there is no base-generated operator in COMP in (80b). The crucial assumption required to explain the status of (80b) is that the resumptive pronoun is not $\bar{A}$-bound at S-structure. Suppose further that the head of the NP in (80b) (namely, *el reloj*) is an NP in an $\bar{A}$-position that has an index at LF (as required, for example, by the discussion of note 11); if this is not the case, no further discussion is required. This internal NP, the head of the full NP, is the only possible $\bar{A}$-binder for the resumptive pronoun. Therefore, it must be that it is not coindexed with the resumptive pronoun at S-structure. Presumably, the index of this internal NP is derived by percolation from the full NP of which it is the head. Then the required conclusion will follow if either (i) the percolation of this index takes place after S-structure, or (ii) the index of the resumptive pronoun is distinct from that of the full NP at S-structure. Either (i) or (ii) (or both) would follow from the assumption that the condition barring an index i within a category indexed i (see note 14) applies at S-structure. There are, then, a variety of plausible assumptions from which it would follow, as required, that the resumptive pronoun is not $\bar{\text{A}}$-bound at S-structure, thus explaining the status of (80b). In this case, a language has the resumptive pronoun strategy if it permits a base-generated pronoun to be coindexed with the head of the NP by the predication rule that applies to LF, along the lines discussed in note 11. Again, an EC resumptive pronoun in a pro-drop language is restricted to positions permitted by the pro-drop parameter, which applies at S-structure.

This accounts for almost everything we have so far noted, but not quite everything. We still have no explanation for the fact that in such constructions as (79), ...*e*...*e*... may occur in place of the expected . . . *him* . . . *him* . . . . The argument so far allows only for the double resumptive pronoun, while excluding the case of one resumptive pronoun licensing a parasitic gap. The double-*e* constructions are permitted, though, and in fact seem more acceptable than the double-*him* constructions. This fact cannot be accounted for within the framework of our assumptions as so far formulated. Therefore, either these assumptions are wrong in some respect, or something else is involved in the double-*e* constructions, perhaps some process involving a strong parallelism requirement, perhaps guided by the Avoid Pronoun Principle. I suspect that the latter may be the case. Some evidence supporting this conjecture is provided by such examples as (82), noted by Luigi Rizzi:

(82)
a.   questa teoria non si puo insegnare t [senza capire e]
     'this theory cannot be taught [without understanding (it)]'
b.   *questa teoria non si puo insegnare t [senza aver capito e]
     'this theory cannot be taught [without having understood (it)]'
c.   una teoria che non puoi insegnare t [senza aver capito e]
     'a theory that you cannot teach [without having understood (it)]'

Examples (82a) and (82b) are very close structurally, but differ in grammatical status. Each one is a construction of the form (57) that we have been considering throughout:

(57)
...α...t...e..., where α binds t and e but t does not c-command e

In (82a,b), α is the initial NP (*questa teoria*), which is in the subject position, moved from the position of t. Therefore, these cannot be parasitic gap constructions, for reasons already discussed. In contrast, (82c) is a normal parasitic gap construction, with α of (57) being the relative operator in COMP binding t and e. Whatever the process may be that forms (82a), it appears to be highly sensitive to parallelism of structure, as (82a,b) and a range of similar examples indicate. As (82c) shows, the defect of (82b) does not reside in the internal structure of the bracketed phrase, but presumably arises from the difference of tense between the matrix clause and the adjunct *senza*-phrase.

The rough English translations appear to reflect a similar phenomenon, though English requires the overt pronoun object in the embedded clause. Many interesting questions arise involving these constructions in English and the Romance languages which I do not understand and will not attempt to pursue here. However, the examples do appear to indicate that a structure of the form (57) may arise even though it is not a parasitic gap construction, apparently with some kind of strong parallelism constraint. It may be that the double-e constructions of (79) are of a similar type, though the facts and their interpretation remain obscure.

Notice that the examples of (82) support the standard view that such constructions as (82a) and (82b) are formed by movement of the matrix object into subject position rather than, as might be suggested, to a position outside S by some form of topicalization. If the latter were true, $\overline{A}$-binding would hold throughout and there would be no reason for a distinction between (82b) and (82c).

Another question that arises in connection with (81) is why e cannot be PRO in a control structure at LF, becoming a variable by coindexing with *wh*- at the LF level, as in (83):

(83)
who$_i$ did John try [e_i to win]

The meaning would be 'for which person x, John tried for x to win'. It is most unlikely that (83) is excluded on semantic grounds. In fact, such examples, with the meaning that (83) would have if it were grammatical, are grammatical in dialects of English that do not observe the *[For-To] Filter (however this is formulated); see Chomsky and Lasnik (1977). The question is why (83) cannot be base-generated as such (abstracting from Subject–Auxiliary Inversion); e would then be PRO at S-structure, satisfying the binding theory, and a variable at LF after LF-indexing of *who*. This relates to a similar question: why cannot such examples as (83) or (84a,b) be formed by ordinary *Wh* Movement in the syntax?

(84)

a. who$_i$ does it seem [t_i to win the race]
b. who$_i$ is it possible [t_i [t_i to win the race]]   (by successive cyclic movement)

In Chomsky (1981a), as above, it is suggested that a θ-role is assigned to a chain, where a chain consists of an element in an A-position and its traces (if any). Furthermore, a chain is "visible" to θ-role assignment only if it has Case or is headed by PRO. In (84), the chain in each case is (t_i), the variable subject of the most deeply embedded clause; since it lacks Case, no θ-role is assigned and the θ-Criterion is violated at LF. The same argument explains why (83) is blocked at LF, though it satisfies the binding theory, with e = PRO, at S-structure. It follows, then, that e in (81) cannot be PRO in a control position at S-structure.

Another problem involves strong crossover under the resumptive pronoun strategy. A consequence of the approach just outlined is that there will be no strong crossover violations involving resumptive pronouns. Consider (85), for example, where we assume *he* and *him* to be coindexed:

(85)

the man who he thought that if Mary marries him, then everyone will be happy

Compare the analogous form (8c), where *him* is taken to be a resumptive pronoun. Presumably, (85) would be permitted in a language or English dialect having a full-fledged resumptive pronoun strategy, but with *he* understood as the variable (in accordance with the definition of *variable* given above) and *him* an ordinary pronominal. It might be that (85) is barred under the intended interpretation by the Avoid Pronoun Principle, since the alternative option (86) is possible:

(86)

the man who t thought that if Mary marries him, then everyone will be happy

In (86), t is the $\overline{A}$-bound variable and *him* is an ordinary pronoun. In short, resumptive pronouns are used only where they must be used to avoid a bounding theory violation.

So far I have been assuming that in (57) (repeated below (82)), t licenses a parasitic gap if and only if α is in an $\overline{A}$-position. Actually, inspection of the argument that led to this conclusion shows that in fact only a slightly weaker conclusion is warranted: for t to license a parasitic gap, α must not receive a θ-role from both t and $e;$ it must not head two chains, (α, t) and (α, e), for if it does, either the θ-Criterion will be violated or e will be wrongly identified as PRO. Thus, compare (87a) with (87b):

(87)
a. the books that they sold t without reading e
b. the books can be sold t without reading e

In (87a), α is the vacuous operator in COMP; it does not head a chain to which a θ-role is assigned, and the construction is therefore acceptable as a parasitic gap construction. In (87b), α ($=$ *the books*) is in subject position; it heads two chains, namely, (*the books*, t) and (*the books, e*), each of which is assigned a θ-role. The θ-Criterion is violated or e is governed PRO, and the construction is completely ungrammatical. Correspondingly, in (87a) α is in an $\overline{A}$-position, while in (87b) it is in an A-position. Note that the problem with (87b) is not that the PRO subject of the *without*-phrase lacks a controller. Thus, the construction is grammatical with *them* in place of $e;$ see (65d).

Suppose, however, that in some construction an element in an $\overline{A}$-position does have a θ-role transmitted to it by a coindexed t. Taking this element to be α in (57), we would expect a parasitic gap construction to be ungrammatical even though α is in an $\overline{A}$-position, by the same θ-Criterion argument that explains the status of (87b). Clitic constructions are of this type. Consider (88):

(88)
Gianni lo vede e
'Gianni sees him'

Here e is an EC in object position, coindexed with the clitic *lo*. The position filled by e is a θ-position, but it seems reasonable to suppose that the clitic *lo* is an argument that requires a θ-role. Therefore, the pair (*lo, e*) is a chain that is assigned a θ-role, the θ-role being transmitted from *e* to *lo* as in the case of NP Movement. However, the clitic *lo* is in an $\bar{A}$-position. We would expect, then, that the EC associated with the clitic should not license a parasitic gap. That is, assuming *lo* in (88) to be α of (57) and *e* to be *t* of (57), we should not be able to form a parasitic gap construction by adding an appropriate phrase with a base-generated EC. The prediction can be tested only if *lo* c-commands the proposed parasitic gap. Luigi Rizzi (to whom these observations are due) suggests the following examples:

(89)
a. i libri che gli dobbiamo far mettere *t* nello scaffale [invece di lasciare *e* sul tavolo]
   'the books that we must make him put on the shelf instead of leaving on the table'

b. glieli dobbiamo far mettere *t* nello scaffale [invece di lasciare *e* sul tavolo]
   'we must make him put them on the shelf instead of leaving (them) on the table'

Example (89a) is grammatical, (89b) ungrammatical. To simplify, I have omitted the EC associated with the clitic *gli* 'him'.

In essentials, the relevant structure is (90):

(90)

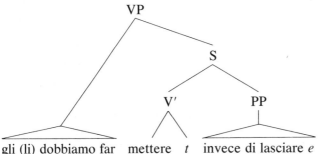

gli (li) dobbiamo far   mettere   *t*   invece di lasciare *e*

In (89a), *t* is $\bar{A}$-bound by an operator in COMP that also binds *e;* therefore, the parasitic gap construction is acceptable, as in earlier discussion. In (89b), however, *t* is $\bar{A}$-bound by the clitic *li* (of *glieli*). Since the clitic c-commands *t*, it also c-commands (hence binds) *e*. It is therefore a structure of the form (57), with α = *li* binding both *t* and *e*. Even though α is in an $\bar{A}$-position, however, the construction is ungrammatical. The clitic *li* heads two chains, (*li, t*) and (*li, e*); *li* receives a dual θ-role, from *t* and from *e,* and the θ-Criterion is violated exactly as in (87b) (note that *e* is not determined to be PRO here, since *li* is in an $\overline{\text{A}}$-position). Further consequences might be explored with regard to the nature of c-command; see note 14. In work in progress, Denis Bouchard explores the possibility that such constructions are barred on the assumption that the clitic, being in an $\overline{\text{A}}$-position, is indexed only at LF. Still other possibilities will be suggested by the discussion in section 5.

We began with the descriptive statement that a parasitic gap is licensed by a variable that does not c-command it. This was modified to the condition that a parasitic gap is licensed by a locally $\overline{\text{A}}$-bound EC that neither c-commands nor is c-commanded by it. We have now seen that such an EC may fail to license a parasitic gap, namely, if it is the EC locally $\overline{\text{A}}$-bound by a clitic. Thus, we have arrived at the descriptive statement (91):

(91)
In the construction (A), where order is irrelevant and we assume α, t, e to be coindexed, the parasitic gap *e* is licensed if and only if (B):

(A) ...α...*t*...*e*...
(B) (i) α c-commands *t* and *e*
    (ii)   *t* does not c-command *e* or conversely
    (iii) α does not head the chains (α, t) and (α, e)
    (iv)   *e* is governed ($\neq$ PRO) and heads a chain with a θ-role

If α is in COMP, as in most of the acceptable examples discussed, then (91Biii) is satisfied, since α heads no chain at all for the purposes of θ-role assignment. If α is in an A-position, then (91Biii) or (91Biv) is always violated, since α heads the chains (α, t) and (α, e), or *e* is PRO (depending on which of the previously outlined arguments we follow). If α is a clitic, then even though it is in an $\overline{\text{A}}$-position, (91Biii) is violated since α heads the chains (α, t) and (α, e). Chains headed by an element α that is either a clitic or in an A-position are eligible for θ-role assignment. The chain will receive a θ-role if exactly one of its terms is in a θ-position and if the chain has Case or α = PRO, as noted earlier; cf. Chomsky (1981a) for further discussion.

The descriptive statement (91) is fairly complex, but this fact is of no interest or concern since it has no independent status but is simply a consequence of quite general principles. Similarly, it is of no significance that the descriptive statement of the distributional properties of gaps (cf. the discussion of (19)) was quite complex; again, it followed from the interaction of simple general principles. Part of the interest of such examples is, in fact, that the descriptive statements are fairly complex and thus can hardly be part of the particular grammar or in anything like direct correspondence to the relevant principles of UG. We expect, then, that in such instances we are observing the consequences of the interaction of simple general principles; and this appears to be the case. As far as (91) is concerned, the predictions are borne out over a rather interesting range, though numerous problems remain, some of which have already been mentioned, some of which are implicit in the specific choice of examples.

One problem that requires discussion is posed by a comparison of (90) with (67), repeated here:

(67)
John offended t by not recognizing e immediately, his favorite uncle from Cleveland

Here α is *his favorite uncle from Cleveland;* it is in an $\overline{\text{A}}$-position, and the relation of α, t, e must satisfy (91), since the construction is grammatical. Satisfaction of (91Bi,ii,iv) is straightforward, but (91Biii) raises a question. Why does α in (67) fail to receive a dual θ-role from t and e, even though li in (90), which is also in an $\overline{\text{A}}$-position, does receive a dual θ-role from t and e? Apparently (α, t) constitutes a chain to which a θ-role is assigned in (67), since the rightward shifted NP (α) receives its θ-role from t. The question then reduces to this: why does (α, e) not constitute a chain in (67)? Or alternatively: why does (α, t) constitute a chain in (67)?

Of these two questions, the second appears to be the appropriate one. Apart from base-generated pairs (clitic, e), a chain is always headed by an element in an A-position; hence, there is no reason to expect (α, e) to constitute a chain in (67). This observation suffices to account for the status of (67) as a parasitic gap construction, since (91Biii) is satisfied, but it leaves open the question of θ-role assignment to α = *his favorite uncle from Cleveland.* It is not too surprising that the question should arise in this case. As has often been noted, Heavy NP Shift is a rule that is not easily incorporable—or, presumably, properly incorporated—within core grammar, for a number of reasons: first, because the concept "heaviness" cannot be expressed within the conceptual framework of core grammar; and second, because the rule adjoins a phrase to a category containing this phrase, a possibility that one might want to rule out in principle for core processes and that in fact cannot be stated within the formalism of earlier and richer versions of the theory of transformations. Similar questions may arise in connection with more central processes such as normal NP Inversion to the right in the pro-drop languages, or with Stylistic Inversion in French. In these and similar cases an NP is adjoined in an $\bar{\text{A}}$-position that is not a base-generated position (as is the position of *li* in (90)) but is instead created by the movement rule. In such cases, the moved element and its trace constitute a chain for the purposes of Case and θ-role assignment, alongside chains headed by an element in an A-position or by a clitic. If this is correct, it follows that chains cannot be "read off of S-structure" but involve the derivation by which S-structure is formed, at least in the case of Heavy NP Shift and possibly in the case of NP Inversion in the pro-drop languages and other processes. There are various ramifications that might be pursued, but again I will leave the matter here, assuming tentatively that a chain is formed by movement to an $\bar{\text{A}}$-position that is not base-generated.

A number of minor technical problems remain. For example, it is necessary to exclude the possibility that base-generated operators in COMP may pick up an index by COMP-to-COMP movement in the syntax, thus binding a base-generated EC at S-structure, causing island violations. The natural proposal for this case is that movement cannot "create" indices but can only carry over indices already assigned, excluding the unwanted possibility since the base-generated operator is only assigned an index at LF. There are a number of other questions of a similar nature. An attempt at full-scale formalization of the relevant assumptions might be in order, given the level of complexity of the range of material that must be considered.

We have seen that an element in COMP has an index at S-structure and hence is a binder just in case it has been moved to this position. Thus, a further distinction is established between S-structure and LF, since at LF such elements may be $\bar{\text{A}}$-binders, as in the case of resumptive pronouns. This is of some interest, since it is a nontrivial matter to justify the existence and distinctness of abstract levels of representation such as LF and S-structure. Also, an additional property must be associated with the complex (46) that defines the syntactic transformation Move α: namely, coindexing in the syntax at S-structure. It is immaterial that control cases also may exhibit coindexing at S-structure, just as it is immaterial that some control cases observe Subjacency. It is the necessary fulfillment of the complex (46), now extended to include coindexing, that characterizes the syntactic rule Move α, i.e. the rule Move α of the syntactic component. This extension is independent of whether Move α is regarded as a rule mapping D-structure to S-structure or as a property of S-structure relating it to a "pure" representation of GF-θ. The discussion above adopted the former interpretation. Assuming the latter, we could presumably recast essentially the same account as a system of conditions on S-structure. Note also that the complex (46), now extended to include coindexing, characterizes the transformational rule Move α of the *syntax,* i.e. of (1Bii). The rule Move α might also apply in the LF and PF components and apparently does, at least in the LF component. There, it is only necessary that Move α obey the ECP, the condition that the antecedent be in a $\bar{\theta}$-position (the latter requirement following from the θ-Criterion), and, of course, coindexing.

In a parasitic gap construction of the form (57), the relation between α and t is a case of Move α. What about the relation between α and e? This relation satisfies all of the properties of the complex associated with Move α apart from those of the bounding theory. Where these are satisfied, as in (11), we do not know which of the two positions, t or e, is the base position of the phrase in COMP. There are some terminological questions to be resolved in such cases involving the concept of Move α and its application, but it does not seem that anything of particular substance is involved.

Unresolved questions arise, however, concerning the relation between α and e in the configuration (81), repeated here, where there is no licensing trace t and α might be, say, a *wh*-phrase:

(81)
α [...e...]

While I have no satisfactory solution to suggest, I will outline some of the problems that remain open.

As noted earlier, the questions that arise do not directly involve the parasitic gap constructions that we have been discussing but rather concern a proper understanding of the resumptive pronoun strategy. The question is why empty resumptive pronominals cannot freely violate island conditions, as would be possible if (81) were to be generated as such without movement and coindexed at S-structure. I have been assuming, therefore, that Ā-positions are not indexed at S-structure by the free indexing procedure, an assumption that so far seems quite well supported. Additional confirming evidence comes from comparison of such sets as (92a–c):

(92)
a. *John filed the article without reading *e*
b. I wonder which article John filed *t* without reading *e*
c. *I wonder who *t* filed the article without reading *e*

Examples (92a) and (92b) are the familiar ones. However, the status of (92c) deserves further comment. We might ask why it cannot be interpreted as in (93), where *who* satisfies the selectional requirement for *wonder:*

(93)
I wonder [O_i who$_j$ [t_j filed the article without reading e_i]]

In (93), the vacuous operator O Ā-binds *e*, while *who* Ā-binds *t*. The problem with (93) cannot be that there are two distinct operators binding variables in the embedded clause; this is standard at LF in the case of multiple *wh*-questions such as (94), which has the LF representation (94b):

(94)
a. I wonder who left without reading what
b. I wonder [what$_i$ who$_j$ [t_j left without reading t_i]]

There is good reason for assuming such representations, whatever the precise character of the operator–S construction at LF, the proper method of resolving the apparent problems of c-command that arise, etc.; see Aoun, Hornstein, and Sportiche (1981) for some recent discussion. There is little reason for supposing S-structure to be different from LF in the relevant respects, so that a representation such as (93) should not violate S-structure conditions.

It might be argued that (93) is excluded by the prohibition against "free variables", in the sense of the discussion of (40). Thus, since *e* in (93) is bound by a vacuous operator, its value must be fixed by an NP-antecedent outside the scope of this operator (namely, *I* in (93)), which gives a senseless interpretation. That cannot be the source of the problem, though, as we can see by replacing *reading* by *meeting*. Then (93) should, under these assumptions, have the sense of (95):

(95)
I wonder who filed the article without meeting me

It is clear, however, that this (perfectly sensible) interpretation is not the sense of this modification of (93). Therefore, (93) must be blocked on other grounds.

One possibility is that (93) is blocked by a requirement of homogeneity for operators in a single COMP. Another is that (93) is blocked on the assumption that the position of *e* is inaccessible to movement and that a base-generated operator *O* in an $\bar{\text{A}}$-position cannot be indexed at S-structure. Given this assumption, at S-structure either $i \neq j$ in (93) so that e_i is governed PRO, or $i = j$ so that again *e* is governed PRO, bound by *t*. This would provide further evidence that free indexing is restricted to A-positions at S-structure.

While this assumption seems quite well supported by the various considerations so far adduced, nevertheless it is somewhat problematic. Before turning to this matter, let me stress again that it appears to have no bearing on the question of parasitic gap constructions. Thus, suppose that contrary to what we have assumed, operators base-generated in $\bar{\text{A}}$-positions can be indexed at S-structure. Nevertheless, they cannot be indexed at S-structure if another operator is present, as we see from (93), whatever the reason may be. Therefore, if there is a "real gap" *t* in the sense of the earlier discussion, the parasitic gap *e* must fall under the operator α that binds *t*, not some independent operator, so that the earlier discussion still stands exactly as before. With this in mind, let us now turn to the question of indexing at S-structure, looking at some new problems.

I have described the positions of parasitic gaps as being in general "relatively inaccessible" to movement. On this assumption, consider again the examples (96a–d) (= (69a–d)), as well as other parasitic gap constructions such as (97a–c):

(96)
a. here is the influential professor that John sent his book to *t* in order to impress *e*
b. this is the type of book that no one who has read *e* would give *t* to his mother

c. he is a man whom everyone who meets *e* admires *t*

d. who did your interest in *e* surprise *t*

(97)

a. the article that I filed *t* without reading *e*

b. the book that I bought *t* because I liked *e*

c. the man that I met *t* without speaking to *e*

Suppose that in (96) and (97) we eliminate the "real gap" *t*, as in (98) and (99):

(98)

a. here is the influential professor that John went to college in order to impress *e*

b. this is the type of book that no one who has read *e* would go to college

c. he is a man whom everyone who meets *e* is sorry

d. who did your interest in *e* surprise Bill

(99)

a. the article that I went to England without reading *e*

b. the book that I went to college because I liked *e*

c. the man that I went to England without speaking to *e*

The examples of (98), (99) range in acceptability from fairly high (e.g. (99a)) to virtual gibberish (e.g. (98d)). Comparing these examples with their parasitic gap counterparts in (96) and (97), we see that they are generally less acceptable than their analogues, sometimes much less so. The relative unacceptability of (98), (99) might be explained on the assumption that the position of the trace of movement (namely, *e* in (98), (99)) is relatively inaccessible to movement under the theory of bounding, the assumption adopted in the earlier discussion of these cases. The question of relative accessibility would then reduce to a class of problems in the theory of bounding that are understood in varying degrees.

However, this assumption is not correct, as Adriana Belletti has observed. The position of the trace *e* in (98) is not "relatively inaccessible to movement", but instead appears to be absolutely inaccessible. We can see this by comparing these examples to similar ones that involve movement of PP (or other cases of "pied piping") to COMP. Thus, compare (99c) with (100):

(100)
the man to whom I went to England without speaking *e*

If the position of the trace in (99c) were only relatively inaccessible to movement, then (100) should have the same status as (99c). But it does not; (100) is unacceptable, while (99c) is relatively acceptable. Similar examples can readily be constructed to illustrate the same point with regard to the other constructions of (98), (99). We conclude, then, that movement is impossible in these constructions. Therefore, the EC *e* is base-generated as such in these constructions and is not the trace of movement. This leaves the problem of accounting for the fact that at least some of the examples of (98), (99) are fairly acceptable. A number of possible solutions come to mind, though each leaves certain questions unresolved.

One possibility, perhaps the most attractive one, is to pursue the line of reasoning of note 11, taking relative clause constructions to involve a kind of predication. Then the LF representation of (99a), for example, would be (101):

(101)
[$_{NP}$ the article]$_i$ [$_{S'}$ that [$_S$ I went to England without reading e_j]]

We assume here that the full NP is indexed *i* at S-structure and that its index percolates to its head (*the article*). The EC of the relative clause is base-generated as an empty pronominal and freely indexed at S-structure. If $j \neq i$, then the construction is barred by the presence of governed PRO.

In the discussion of resumptive pronouns following (81), I assumed that the index of e_j must be distinct from *i* at S-structure and that percolation of the index *i* to the head of the relative clause must take place after S-structure. I suggested that these results would follow from the assumption that the principle barring an index *i* within a construction with the index *i* holds at S-structure. We can, of course, allow percolation to be permitted anywhere, though barred by this principle if it takes place at S-structure. Suppose now that under certain conditions C, the barrier to *i*-within-*i* indexing is relaxed. Then (101) is permitted at S-structure with $j = i$, assuming that (101) meets the conditions C. Now *e* is Ā-bound by the head of the full NP, assuming that the position of the head is an Ā-position, as is not implausible; various questions remain open regarding the proper interpretation of θ-marking and the θ-Criterion in the case of relative clauses, and one of the possible solutions does involve this assumption. These assumptions amount to interpreting the EC in (98), (99) as a kind of resumptive pronominal. It would still follow that resumptive pronouns do not license parasitic gaps, as we have seen to be the case, if these constructions do not satisfy the conditions C.

What might these conditions be? Comparison of the relatively acceptable (99a) with the unacceptable (98d), and in general of similar examples, suggests that there may be a certain value in the suggestion of Chomsky and Lasnik (1977), (also, in another connection, Williams (1978)) that some kind of "deletion" operation is possible with a left – right asymmetry, preferring elements that are further to the right in a construction. See also the problems posed by such examples as (82) and (70).

It remains, of course, to determine the nature of the conditions C. Even supposing that this can be done, further questions arise. For example, there should be a contrast between relatives and interrogatives. Thus, while (99a), for example, should be acceptable, the corresponding interrogatives (e.g. (98d) or (102)) should not.

(102)
which article did you go to England without reading

While this conclusion seems to me correct for (98d), it does not seem correct for (102), though perhaps this example is somewhat less acceptable than (99a). It also follows that under the conditions C, parasitic gap constructions would no longer violate the Bijection Principle and should be fully acceptable, and that under the conditions C we should find weak crossover violations in relative clauses (see note 11). It is difficult to evaluate these consequences.

Other possible approaches to this problem come to mind, but they seem to raise the same difficulties in addition to others. For example, it might be supposed that for some reason movement-to-COMP is possible in these cases but not pied piping, or that indexing of $\overline{A}$-positions at S-structure is possible in these cases (but not when an operator is already present, as we have seen in the case of (93), so that this possibility does not affect the matter of parasitic gaps). Exactly the same questions now present themselves, along with the question of why these further discrepancies should arise.

For the reasons already discussed, it is once again to be expected that the right answer to these questions, whatever it is, will not involve special rules of particular grammar or special principles of UG specific to these constructions, but will simply follow from independent principles of UG (or perhaps some other system) and specific properties of the constructions involved, as we have seen to be the case over a substantial range of parasitic gap constructions. These problems may prove to be interesting ones, depending on what the operative principles turn out to be.

Returning now to parasitic gap constructions, the phenomenon illustrates once again, I think in quite an interesting way, how the study of ECs proves to be a useful probe into structures and an important test for theory. It also shows how simple and quite plausible principles interact to explain some fairly complex phenomena for which we have every reason to believe there are no specific rules either of particular or universal grammar.

There is a familiar moral to the story that should not be obscured in the technical details. The moral I think is correct, even if the story turns out to be wrong. A descriptive statement such as (56) or (58) does not resolve the problem of parasitic gaps; rather, it poses the problem. The problem is to explain why the phenomenon exists with the properties it has. For the reasons discussed earlier, the answer is very likely to be that the phenomenon exists with the properties it has because of other properties of UG and the particular grammar that are quite independent of parasitic gaps; again, it is most unlikely that particular grammars have rules governing parasitic gaps or that UG includes specific principles bearing on this phenomenon, which is a particularly interesting one for just this reason. While this seems a very plausible assumption, it amounts to quite a strong claim, as noted earlier. It means, for example, that all of the quite intricate properties of parasitic gaps must be reducible to general principles of UG, given rules and structures of the particular grammar that are established on other grounds; it means as well that if languages appear to differ with respect to the existence or properties of parasitic gaps, these differences must be completely explained on the basis of other structural differences among the languages in question. The task for the linguist, then, is to show how independent principles of UG and independent properties of a particular grammar interact to yield the distribution and interpretation of parasitic gaps. It is very likely that an attempt to do this—for example, the attempt just undertaken—will fail; additional cases will be discovered in the language in question showing that it is defective, or the principles invoked will prove to yield incorrect results in other languages. Such failure is likely precisely because the endeavor is a nontrivial one. Suppose that counterevidence is discovered—as we should expect and as we should in fact hope, since precisely this eventuality will offer the possibility of a deeper understanding of the real principles involved. The conclusion will not be that particular grammars or UG contain specific descriptive principles governing parasitic gaps, but rather that we do not yet understand the relevant principles of UG or the relevant properties of the language in question, as is surely likely to be the case. In a field that is alive and concerned with nontrivial questions, one naturally expects that assumptions and ideas will change as more is learned, particularly so in a newly emerging discipline that has only quite recently even posed, let alone undertaken, the fundamental questions of explanation.

A similar moral should be drawn in other cases as well, for example, in the interpretation of such structures as (40). Again, it is hard to believe that the interpretation follows either from principles of UG specific to these structures or from language-specific rules of particular grammar. The task, then, is to show how the facts follow from general principles of UG and independent properties of the language in question. Or consider such phenomena as cliticization. There is every reason to suppose that the language-specific rule relating to clitics is that a clitic may be related to an arbitrary NP position (with, perhaps, some parametric variation). The many curious properties of clitics should then follow from general principles of UG, given other structural features of the language. Similarly, in the case of anaphors and pronominals, we hardly expect to find language-specific rules apart from the rule (perhaps, lexical property) that an item is an anaphor or pronominal (e.g. *each other, he*), with perhaps some restricted parametric variation. It is in fact this assumption that has motivated work in binding theory for the past ten years, leading to successive refinements and improvements as simpler and more natural principles have been discovered and the range of relevant data sharpened and extended. Or, in the case of marginal phenomena such as the *wanna* contraction in English, we surely expect that the rule is simply that *want-to* becomes *wanna* optionally. The question becomes interesting, and worth pursuing, precisely when this rule appears to fail; in this case, the failure leads to further inquiry, and we hope insight, into the principles involved. If this simple rule fails in such cases as (103a,b), we do not conclude that there is some more complex description of the rule of contraction, but rather that there are general principles of UG that explain why the failure is only apparent.

(103)
a. who do you want *t* to see Bill
b. they want, to be sure, a place in the sun

In (103a), the answer seems to be that Case makes an EC visible for certain types of phonological rule, perhaps a subcase of a more general Visibility Principle as suggested in connection with (83), (84). Regarding (103b), the answer presumably lies in a proper understanding of the domain for certain types of phonological process, a notion that may in part be a reflex of syntactic properties of government and the like. The same is true in many other cases.

Analogous considerations apply elsewhere. Suppose, for example, that a theory of cliticization builds in principles that permit cliticization from infinitives but not finite clauses, or that the special devices of some theory of passives make a similar distinction. These are not to be construed as positive achievements, but rather as negative results, that is, as arguments against the proposed theories. The theory of cliticization or passivization should not single out the position of subject of an infinitive, but should rather permit these processes to operate quite freely (contrary to fact). The reason is implicit in our earlier discussion. These properties of clitics and of the passive construction reflect independent principles that hold of overt anaphors and pronominals. A theory of clitics or passives that specifically provides for these facts is therefore missing what appears to be an important generalization: namely, that the unfilled position of subcategorization and θ-marking associated with passivization or cliticization shares properties of anaphors and appears to be subject to the general principles that apply to such elements. The task for the linguist, then, is to show that some minimal characterization of the processes involved (perhaps just Move α or the principle that any position can be cliticized) suffices, in interaction with other principles of UG and properties of the grammar in question, to yield the observed phenomena. See also the discussion of (7), (8) in section 1.

In general, it is to be expected that any principled approach to such topics—any attempt to show either that no special rules are involved (as in the case of parasitic gaps), or that the minimal rule suffices (as in the case of cliticization, *wanna*-contraction, or passive), or that a parameter is set one way or another (as in the case of the pro-drop parameter and the various properties that appear to be associated with it)—will fail, at least in part. Correspondingly, we should expect to find continual revision of such proposals as new phenomena are discovered and better insight is obtained into relevant principles. In contrast, some descriptive statement might prove accurate, a fact that would simply indicate the existence of a problem worth studying.

These remarks should be regarded as truisms. A look at recent literature suggests, however, that unfortunately they are not.

5. Binding Theory and the Typology of Empty Categories

I have been discussing some consequences of the more principled approach to ECs in chapter 6 of Chomsky (1981a), which replaces an interpretation in terms of intrinsic content by a functional interpretation. Continuing to rethink the status of ECs, let us consider again Principles A and B of the binding theory, perhaps its only principles.[36] These principles identify two categories of expressions: anaphors and pronominals. Principle A holds of anaphors, Principle B of pronominals. If the binding theory is correct, then in the best of all possible worlds we would expect to find four categories of expressions:

(104)
a. [+anaphor, −pronominal]
b. [−anaphor, +pronominal]
c. [+anaphor, +pronominal]
d. [−anaphor, −pronominal]

In the case of overt categories with lexical content, we do find examples of (104a), (104b), (104d); namely, overt anaphors (*each other*), pronouns (*he*), and R-expressions (*John*), respectively. There could not be an overt element corresponding to (104c), since it would have to be ungoverned by virtue of Principles A and B of the binding theory and would therefore violate the Case Filter.[37] For overt elements, then, the classification in (104) seems reasonable.

Now consider ECs. The most plausible general assumption is that the typology of ECs simply mirrors that of overt categories, that is, that no new principles are invoked to determine the types of EC. We would therefore expect to find ECs of each of the four types (104a–d) (unless some are barred by independent principles), and no other types. Furthermore, if some category of (104) is subdivided for overt elements (for instance, pure pronominals can be referential or pleonastic), we would expect to find the same subdivision for ECs.

How well are these natural expectations realized? We have encountered examples of (a), (c), and (d) of (104): namely, NP-trace, PRO, and variable, respectively. These, in fact, are the three types of EC so far identified. There is no principled reason why there should not be an EC of type (104b), that is, a pronominal nonanaphor satisfying only Principle B of the binding theory.

This gap in the paradigm immediately brings to mind a serious conceptual deficiency of the system outlined in Chomsky (1981a), alluded to in note 22; namely, while the status of pronominal anaphor is quite appropriate for control PRO, it makes no sense for the noncontrol PRO that I assumed in that study to be the "missing subject" in the pro-drop languages. The reason is that this element, while it does share the basic features of pronouns apart from lexical content and the consequences thereof, does not share the basic feature of anaphors, namely, lack of independent reference. Rather, this element either has specific definite reference or serves as a pleonastic element in the manner of English *there, it* or French *il,* in their nonreferential usages. In short, this element functions simply as an empty pronominal, not a pronominal anaphor; it is an EC of the type (104b), exactly as is its overt counterpart. In (105a), for example, the EC *e* is as definite in reference as is *he* in the translation; and in (105b), the EC functions essentially in the same way as the pleonastic element of the translation:

(105)
a. *e* parla
   'he is speaking'
b. *e* arriva un ragazzo
   'there arrives a boy'

The system in Chomsky (1981a) is simply incorrect in taking the EC subject in such cases to be PRO, for this conceptual reason alone. Note that the approach of Rizzi (1980b) does not suffer from this deficiency.

We do not want to interpret the "missing subject" of the pro-drop languages as PRO, but for analogous reasons we do not want to interpret it as trace. Thus, it is neither a pure anaphor analogous to NP-trace (thus, if AGR can serve as its binder, then it should also do so for subject anaphors, yielding NIC violations, under the simplest assumptions) nor a variable analogous to *wh*-trace. Certain descriptive problems are also overcome if this element is taken to be, say, PRO rather than trace. Thus, this element can be moved to subject position, as in (106):

(106)
e fu arrestato *t*
'he was arrested'

Here *t* is the trace left by movement of *e* from the object position, where it is an EC pronominal in D-structure. It is not clear what it would mean, in our terms, to say that *e* is a trace in its S-structure position. To take a more complex example of the same sort, consider the sentences (107a–c):

(107)
a. si mangiano le mele
   'the apples are eaten'
b. le mele si mangiano
   (same)
c. si mangiano
   'they are eaten'

We may assume (107a) to be in its base-generated form, putting aside here the question of why the verb agrees with its object. Example (107b) is derived by Move α; the object moves into subject position, which we may assume to be a $\bar{\theta}$-position, the θ-role of subject being "absorbed" by *si*. Now consider (107c). It should be exactly analogous to (107b) in S-structure and to (107a) in D-structure; that is, it should have the D-structure (108a) and the S-structure (108b) derived from (108a) by Move α:

(108)
a. si mangiano *e*
b. *e* si mangiano *t*

Again these results follow if the EC subject of (107c) is taken to be PRO, but not if it is taken to be trace, which cannot appear at D-structure.

Considerable discussion has recently been devoted to whether the "missing subject" in pro-drop languages is trace, PRO, or some other kind of EC. If the preceding analysis is correct, then the terms of this discussion have been misleadingly chosen throughout. The real questions are: how does the EC in question fall under the classification (104), and what exactly are the mechanisms of agreement, Case assignment, and so forth? The answer to the first question, it seems, is that the EC in (105), in the subject position of (106), (108b), and in the object position of (108a) fills the gap in the paradigm (104); that is, it is a pronominal nonanaphor of type (104b), just like its overt counterpart that alternates with it under various conditions in the pro-drop languages and constitutes the only option in the non-pro-drop languages.

The reason why the question was wrongly posed becomes clear when we consider the recent history of these notions. The notion "PRO" developed from the study of Equi NP deletion and control. The notion "trace" developed from the study of transformational rules. In each case, the concepts developed in a natural way in the course of the continuing effort to restrict the descriptive variety of grammars while maintaining or enhancing the explanatory power of linguistic theory. This evolution left the residual assumption that there are two basic types of EC—namely, PRO and trace—and that the problem is to determine their properties and the principles from which these properties follow. That is the standpoint adopted in many recent studies, including Chomsky (1981a), which I have largely followed here in the earlier discussion. But from the standpoint we have now reached, that approach appears to have been incorrect, a misleading residue of the development of linguistic theory in the past years. From our present point of view, it is the principles of GB theory and the classification of elements they induce (specifically, (104)) that are fundamental. The notions "PRO" and "trace" remain, but as derivative categories. The notion "trace" arises from the theory of Move α. We may continue to use PRO to stand for an EC that has the features [+pronominal, +anaphor] and that enters into the theory of control. We have also identified a new element, call it *pro,* having the features [+pronominal, −anaphor]. In the terminology of Chomsky (1981a), PRO is the EC PRO in an S-structure position ungoverned at D-structure by INFL, hence lacking a superscript, while *pro* is the element designated as PRO^i in an S-structure position governed at D-structure by INFL, now understood to be a pure pronominal like its overt counterpart. There is now no reason why it should not be governed at S-structure as well.

There is empirical support for the latter conclusion. Torrego (1981) points out that Spanish interrogatives involve obligatory verb fronting, placing the subject in a governed position, namely, governed by the fronted verb. This is true of both direct and indirect questions (with some exceptions that we may ignore), as in (109):

(109)

a. con quién podrá Juan ir a Nueva York
   'with whom will Juan be able to go to New York'
b. no me acuerdo a quién prestó Juan el diccionario
   'I don't remember to whom Juan lent the dictionary'

Torrego argues that the position filled by *Juan* is not only governed but also properly governed. It can also be filled by an EC "missing subject" in this pro-drop language, something that is impossible if the EC is taken to be PRO as in Chomsky (1981a) but perfectly possible if the EC is a pure pronominal of the category (104b). The Aux-to-COMP constructions of Italian studied by Rizzi (1981) suggest a similar treatment.

It remains to explain the limited distribution of the EC pure pronominal, specifically, the fact that it is restricted to subject position in the pro-drop languages. We might approach the question in the following way, keeping to a rather intuitive level. There should be some grammatical indication of the presence, type, and content of an EC. The presence of an EC is determined by the Extended Projection Principle. As far as its type is concerned, the problem is to assign each occurrence to one of the categories of (104), and to whatever additional subcategories there may be. The starting point can be formal (beginning with properties of the grammatical structure in which the EC appears and proceeding to determination of its status as [±anaphor], [±pronominal] with the associated semantic role) or semantic (beginning with the semantic function of the EC which determines its status with regard to the binding theory and proceeding to evaluate the status of the construction in question in these terms). The two approaches are, of course, not mutually exclusive. Let us briefly consider each, beginning with the semantically based approach.

The earlier version of the binding theory involved three kinds of category: R-expressions, pronominals, and anaphors. There was one binding principle for each kind of category. Under the revision eliminating

Principle C from the binding theory, there are in principle four kinds of category: R-expression (neither anaphor nor pronominal), pronominal, anaphor, pronominal anaphor (cf. (104)). Notice that when we assign an expression to one of these categories, we are considering it as an occurrence of a type (a certain class of tokens). Thus, for instance, *he* is a pronominal with respect to the binding theory, not an R-expression, even if it is functioning as a variable under the resumptive pronoun strategy. Thus, to categorize expressions according to this approach, we first take them to be tokens of a certain type, then ask what the category of this type is (R-expression, etc.), and finally turn to the application of the binding theory and other principles.

We can proceed roughly in the following fashion. Suppose that we assume some domain D of "entities", which are accorded no ontological status (apart from mental representation); for reasons I will not discuss here, I believe that this assumption is also required to make sense of other approaches (e.g. model-theoretic approaches) to what is misleadingly called "natural language semantics". Consider first singular expressions. An R-expression is one that inherently selects an element of D in the following sense: if overt, it denotes an element of D by virtue of its inherent properties; if nonovert, it is a variable ranging over a subset of D determined by the inherent properties of the restriction on its operator, or if there is no restriction, taking as value the element of D denoted by its NP-antecedent in the manner described earlier. A pronominal selects an element of D in a similar way, but not by virtue of its inherent properties (apart from the restriction to a subset of D determined by its grammatical features). A pronominal may denote an element of D as determined by a linguistic antecedent or some contextual indication, or it may function as a variable under the resumptive pronoun strategy. Thus, a pronominal is an element that may in effect serve as an R-expression, given an appropriate context, though the function of a pronominal as a potential R-expression is not determined by the overt–EC distinction. A pure pronominal is an element that must become an R-expression in the sense just indicated, either denoting an element of D or ranging over a subset of D as determined by the restriction on its operator. Turning to anaphors, an anaphor is an element that may fail to denote. A pure anaphor is one that always fails to denote but is, in effect, interpreted as a variable assigned a value by virtue of its relation to its antecedent. A pronominal anaphor, then, exploits the options available to pronominals and anaphors: it may denote as determined by context (bound PRO), or it may function as a "free variable" lacking an operator (free PRO with arbitrary interpretation; cf. Chomsky (1981b)). Precisely in the latter case, the principle assigning values to variables with empty operators will be vacuous, since there is no operator. We can extend the same analysis to plurals, taking denotation to be either multiple denotation of individuals or denotation of sets. Extension to elements with variables as antecedents is straightforward. To ensure that pleonastic elements (e.g. *it* in *it is clear that S*) are pure pronominals, not anaphors, we may assume that D contains a designated element that they denote. Proceeding along these lines, we may assign expressions to their categories, then applying the binding theory and other principles to the constructions in which they appear.

Let us now consider the alternative approach, thus in effect reasoning from properties of the construction in which an expression appears to determination of its status in the typology of (104), hence its "semantic" function. We may now limit attention to ECs, assuming that inherent lexical features determine the categorization of an overt element. Suppose that the EC is locally bound by an element in a $\bar{\theta}$-position. Then it is [−pronominal], either [−anaphor] if the local binder is in an $\bar{A}$-position or [+anaphor] if the local binder is in an A-position. (However, see notes 4, 11, 17, 18.) Suppose that the EC is free or locally bound by an element in a θ-position. Then it is [+pronominal], just as in the case of an overt category with these properties. The next step is to determine whether the element is [+anaphor] or [−anaphor]. This step depends on some theory-internal decisions that are not entirely clear. Various possibilities might be pursued, though it should be borne in mind that there is no real need for a determinate heuristic. The simplest option is to assume that the feature [±anaphor] is assigned to the element arbitrarily, other principles then determining whether the choice was valid. It will follow that the feature [+anaphor] can be selected only in an ungoverned position, the alternative being ruled out by the binding theory. Then in all cases, the type of the EC is determined as [±anaphor], [±pronominal].

Given this information, we can establish chains (or perhaps they are determined by the derivation, as suggested in the discussion following (91)). If a pronominal (whether overt or an EC) is in a chain containing a distinct argument, it is pleonastic; otherwise, it is an argument. The remaining properties of chains discussed earlier must also be satisfied, along with other conditions, for a structure containing an EC to be well formed. Recall that if certain conditions (e.g. the "weak" Bijection Principle) are relaxed, the construction still exhibits a range of quite specific and determinate properties.

We may continue to refer to the element [+pronominal, +anaphor] as PRO and to the element [+pronominal, −anaphor] as *pro,* taking each of these to be a cover term for various combinations of the "grammatical features" person, gender, number—and possibly also Case. As before, an element that is [−pronominal] is trace, perhaps extending this term now to the EC associated with a clitic.

Turning now to the content of an EC, we continue to assume that it must be somehow determined. The content of trace is determined by the antecedent; and as we have seen in connection with (40), where the antecedent is a null operator there is necessarily a more remote NP-antecedent that determines the grammatical features of trace. The content of PRO is determined by the antecedent if there is one, and is fixed with the arbitrary variable-like interpretation if there is no antecedent.[38] This leaves only *pro.* We want to establish that in the core cases, *pro* appears only as the subject of a sentence with AGR in a pro-drop language. Putting aside the relevant property of AGR for a moment, this will follow if we require that the content of *pro* must not only be determined, but in fact "locally determined", by the AGR element of the thematic complex (the complex of head and arguments; see Rouveret and Vergnaud (1980)) of which it is a part. At D-structure, AGR is part of INFL, governing the subject position; but at S-structure it must be possible for AGR to be attached to the main verb.[39] In essence following Rizzi (1980b), the simplest approach is to understand "local determination" as "government by AGR". If INFL does not attach to the main verb in the syntax, then it governs the subject at S-structure and can determine the content of *pro,* also excluding PRO from this governed position. If INFL does move to the main verb in the syntax, then V-movement to a position governing the subject must be obligatory to block PRO and determine the content of *pro* under government. The technical details can be worked out in various ways. We might think of the condition of "local determination" of content for *pro* as being analogous to a dual property of trace: its content is determined by its antecedent, and its position is locally determined by the ECP and bounding theory. Something similar is true for controlled PRO, which also strongly tends to find an antecedent within the thematic complex in which it appears or in which its clause is an argument.

As for the pro-drop parameter, we may continue to adopt the suggestion of Taraldsen (1978b) in the paper that initiated the recent inquiry into this topic: namely, the possibility of having a pure pronominal EC subject is related, though sometimes imprecisely, to a "rich enough" inflectional system, so that the inflection determines the grammatical features of the "missing subject". We might characterize the notion "rich enough" in terms of Case theory, this being just one of a number of possible alternatives. Thus, the AGR element is a set of specifications for the features person, gender, number, and (in pro-drop languages) Case. The pro-drop parameter reduces then to the question of whether AGR is specified at D-structure for Case, a reasonable option for a complex of grammatical features. If it is, then it is *pro;* if not, it is PRO. There will then be a strong tendency to "spell out" AGR in the PF component if it has Case, perhaps another example of the Visibility Principle. Assuming that agreement involves identity of grammatical features, then in the pro-drop languages the EC subject governed by AGR is *pro* with Case. If this element is introduced into the subject position of a non-pro-drop language, the structure is barred by failure of agreement, that is, its content is not determined. While we assume that in any event AGR assigns nominative Case under government, in the pro-drop languages it does so under strict feature matching, assuming this technical device.

We might restate these points in slightly different terms, following proposals by Osvaldo Jaeggli and Youssef Aoun. Suppose that a pronoun is simply the "spelling out" of a pronominal with Case, i.e. *pro.* In other words, at S-structure we insert the appropriate phonological matrix for a pure pronominal EC with Case.[40] In the non-pro-drop languages, it is always necessary to add this phonological matrix at S-structure; otherwise, the content of the EC will not be properly determined. In a pro-drop language, *pro* with Case can be left in subject position governed by AGR, since its content will be determined by AGR with Case, i.e. the *pro* INFL. We might extend the same ideas to pro-drop languages (e.g. some dialects of Italian) that have subject clitics, regarding these as a "spelling out" of the AGR element and thus different from the subject clitic of, say, French.

In all cases, then, the feature content of an EC is determined. Furthermore, *pro* is restricted in S-structure to the D-structure subject position of a construction with a "rich enough" inflection AGR, though there are other cases to consider which I ignore here; see Rizzi (1980b), Chomsky (1981b).

The requirement of "local determination" for *pro* seems necessary, since the feature content of pleonastic *pro* is, in fact, determined in another way: namely, by properties of the postverbal element with which it is linked. This fact is clear in the pro-drop languages when the EC is raised and the matrix verb agrees with the postverbal element, as in (110), in which the matrix verb is first person singular:

(110)
pro sembro [*t* essere io]
'it seems to be me'

Nevertheless, such nonlocal determination of content evidently does not suffice to permit *pro* subject, or we would find EC pleonastic subjects in the non-pro-drop languages.

Similar ideas can be extended to the EC associated with a clitic. If we assume something like the theory of cliticization developed by Borer (1981), then the clitic governs the associated EC and in fact determines its features as well. The EC associated with the clitic is presumably either an anaphor (as in (104a)) or *pro* (as in (104b)). Since these questions were placed on the research agenda by Kayne (1975), it has been widely assumed that cliticization is subject to the binding conditions for anaphors. Suppose this to be the case, as seems plausible given the fact that the subject of a tensed clause cannot be cliticized, along with other more complex considerations adduced by Kayne, Rouveret and Vergnaud (1980), and others. Then the EC is an anaphor subject to the ECP and Principle A of the binding theory. The clitic itself, then, is presumably a pronominal subject to Principle B of the binding theory. These are basically the conclusions of Borer (1981), contrary to those of Jaeggli (1980), Chomsky (1981a).

If the EC associated with the clitic is taken to be *pro* rather than an anaphor (in effect, NP-trace), the opacity effects might still be obtained on the assumption of Borer (1981) that the EC associated with the clitic must be governed by it (determination of the content of *pro* being contingent on government) and that the preposed verbal phrase in such constructions as Romance causatives is not a VP and hence is not "protected" from government by the clitic in the sense of earlier discussion. This possibility raises many questions that would carry us too far afield.

In either case, some modification is required in the approach just described for determining the type of an EC. In the case of cliticization, the position of the EC is a θ-position; that of the clitic, a $\bar{\theta}$-position (in fact an $\bar{A}$-position). As we have seen earlier, we must apparently assume that the pair (clitic, e) constitutes a chain for the purposes of θ-role assignment. As far as I can see, something has to be stipulated to permit this, as in the earlier discussion. This same stipulation can readily be formulated, in one or another way, to identify the EC associated with the clitic as either [+anaphor] or [+pronominal], depending on the proper resolution of this question.

Consider then the case of clitic doubling. If the clitic and the associated EC or double constitute a chain, then we may assume (following a suggestion of Aoun) that the clitic "absorbs" Case. Furthermore, it may either manifest Case or not. If it does manifest Case, then the chain headed by the clitic has Case and the chain will be (clitic, e). If the clitic does not manifest Case, then some other element of the chain must manifest Case for the chain to be assigned a θ-role, assuming the Visibility Principle. Therefore, the chain must be (clitic, lexical NP), where the lexical NP (the double) must be assigned Case by some independent means (Kayne's generalization). In either case, the chain will have Case and will be subject to θ-marking. A precise version of these assumptions is relatively straightforward.

Adapting the terminology of Chomsky (1981a), let us say that a certain relation SUP, indicated by superscripting, holds of: (i) the subject of a clause and the AGR element that governs it, the superscript being "carried along" by movement of either AGR or the subject; (ii) a clitic and the EC that it governs; (iii) a pleonastic element and the phrase with which it is associated.[41] The content of an EC matches that of an element that bears the relation SUP to it. Every EC must meet one of the following conditions: (I) it is properly governed (trace, under the ECP); (II) it is subject to the theory of control (the pronominal anaphor PRO); or (III) it bears SUP to INFL that is "strong enough" to satisfy the pro-drop parameter, or perhaps to a clitic (pure pronominal pro). The various combinations of Principles A and B of the binding theory provide the basic typology of ECs. Their presence, type, and content are determined in the manner just outlined, and their properties and distribution are further determined by the principles of government, binding and θ-theory. Many questions arise concerning the pro-drop parameter, the nature of agreement, cliticization, control, and other matters.[42] It seems to me, however, that this general approach has much to recommend it.

Many other topics receive a rather natural and often illuminating treatment within the framework of GB theory. Although there are evidently numerous remaining problems and open questions and many alternatives to specific suggestions discussed here and in other related studies, and although the framework is undoubtedly too narrowly restricted to phenomena in certain well-studied languages, nevertheless it seems to me that the theory that is developing has the right kinds of properties and represents a qualitative advance over earlier approaches. I also tend to believe that when the proper level of abstraction is achieved, we will find that some alternative approaches fall together in significant respects with GB theory,[43] although differences remain that it will be important to identify, clarify, and resolve.

The GB theory has a highly modular character. Simple and rather natural principles interact to provide for a variety of fairly complex phenomena, and slight changes in the values of parameters proliferate through the system to yield what appear on the surface to be rather different language structures. These are properties that the correct theory should have, whatever it may turn out to be, given standard poverty of stimulus arguments.

The problem has always been to discover the elements that interact to yield the full complexity of a natural language. Early transformational grammar was in part on the wrong track in attributing this complexity to the variety of phrase structure rules and transformations[44]— in more technical terms, in taking the basic elements to be rewriting rules of the base grammar and the restricting classes and elementary operations of which transformations were composed. The phrase structure rules can be largely and perhaps completely eliminated along the lines sketched earlier, and the components of transformations in the sense of earlier work can be virtually abandoned; they did not have the independent significance that should be manifested by the right choice of basic abstract features, as Heny (1981) observes. I think we may now be a good bit closer to identifying these fundamental elements: principles of the kind I have been outlining, which are now being investigated and developed in work that I think has already been quite fruitful and that raises many intriguing questions for further study.

Notes

1. For more extensive discussion of many topics mentioned here, see Chomsky (1981a) and references cited there. Sections 1 and 2 of this monograph are based on a lecture given at the Sixth Scandinavian Conference of Linguistics, Røros, Norway, June 1981.

2. Examples will be given in conventional notation, with syntactic structure only partially indicated to bear on the matter at hand. I will use the symbol *e* to stand for an empty nominal category, i.e. an NP with no phonological matrix.

3. I will henceforth capitalize *Case* when the term is used in its technical sense.

4. See Chomsky (1981a, chapter 3). In forthcoming work, Youssef Aoun presents evidence that the binding theory also applies at the LF level, and that the ECP can in fact be reduced to the binding theory. See note 11. Michael Brody suggests a different way to achieve the latter result in work now in preparation, as part of a very interesting reconstruction of the principles of GB theory. Kayne (1981a) argues that Subjacency can in large measure be reduced to a somewhat different version of the ECP. It is a question of considerable interest to determine precisely the interconnections among the various concepts and principles of a linguistic theory, though it has only fairly recently become possible to raise the question in a very serious way. Among important earlier contributions along these lines are Freidin's study (1978) of the relation between binding theory and the theory of the cycle, as well as the investigations by Tarald Taraldsen, Richard Kayne, and David Pesetsky into the relations between binding theory and the *[That-*Trace] Filter (now subsumed under the ECP), cited in Chomsky (1981a, chapter 4), which primarily motivated much of the investigation of the concepts of GB theory.

5. However, Case (specifically genitive Case) can perhaps be assigned in other ways. There are unresolved questions concerning the assignment of nominative Case, for example, to postverbal subjects in the pro-drop languages. In Chomsky (1981a, chapter 4), it is suggested that this too is an instance of Case assignment under government; for alternative views, see Rizzi (1980b), Burzio (1981).

6. Or, we might say, the "grammatical component of the language faculty", if the latter is construed in broader terms.

7. For reasons that have frequently been discussed (see, for instance, Chomsky (1980b)), intensive study of particular languages is likely to give deeper insight into UG than less far-reaching study of a wide variety of languages (a conclusion that has sometimes been erroneously regarded as paradoxical), though ultimately of course UG must be developed so as to characterize the notion "possible human language". See Marantz (1981) for important work that combines coverage of a wide variety of language types with construction of a well-articulated theory of UG that is conceptually similar in many respects to the GB theory. Another natural research strategy is to consider languages that differ in some cluster of properties but have developed separately for a relatively short time, so that it is reasonable to suppose that a difference in the values of only a few parameters accounts for the apparent typological difference. Recent work on the syntax of the Romance languages, initiated by Kayne's very important investigations (cf. Kayne (1975) and subsequent studies), exemplifies this approach.

8. Various assumptions have been made concerning the exact form of rule (4a). The version here modifies an approach suggested by Emonds (1976). INFL is the abstract inflectional element, which may be either [+inflection] (tensed) or [−inflection] (infinitival) and which may contain the agreement element AGR (which I will tentatively assume to be identical to PRO, that is, a collection of values for the features person, gender, and number) and presumably modals. For discussion bearing on this matter, see Steele et al. (1981).

9. For discussion of this matter, considerably extending the remarks in Chomsky (1981a), see Stowell (1981). On X-bar theory and the "Greenberg universals", see Graffi (1980).

10. See Koopman and Sportiche (1981), where the Bijection Principle is proposed and other consequences are also discussed. The binding in question is local $\bar{\text{A}}$-binding, in the sense defined below. For further discussion bearing on this matter, see Taraldsen (1979), Engdahl (1981a,b). I return to this topic in section 4.

11. Suppose that this is the case. If so, it is not necessary to impose the requirement that the head of a relative clause is coindexed at LF with the relative pronoun; for example, that in (8a) *the man* is coindexed with *who*. Rather, the general principle of relative clause interpretation that applies to (not prior to) LF will determine that the relative clause, taken as an open sentence, is predicated of the head. For example, suppose that the LF representation of (8a) is (i):

(i)

[the man]$_i$ [who$_j$ John saw t_j]

The rule of Predication, applying to the LF representation (i), identifies i and j, yielding the representation (ii):

(ii)

[the man]$_i$ [who$_i$ John saw t_i]

This yields the interpretation (9), in the obvious way. Let us refer to the representation (ii), derived from the LF representation (i), as an LF′ representation, without prejudicing the question of whether it is actually at a new *level* of representation or whether it is simply a stage in the interpretation of LF, which may involve a number of steps.

Some evidence in support of these assumptions is provided by the weak crossover phenomenon. It is well known that weak crossover effects are suppressed in relative constructions. Compare (iii) with (iv):

(iii)

the man who his mother loved t best

(iv)

who did his mother love t best

The former can be interpreted as (v), but the corresponding interpretation of (iv) as (vi) yields a weak crossover violation:

(v)

the man x such that x's mother loved x best

(vi)

for which person x, x's mother loved x best

Suppose now that we interpret relative clause structures in terms of predication, as suggested. This allows the LF representation (vii) corresponding to (iii):

(vii)

[the man]$_i$ [who$_j$ his$_i$ mother loved t_j best]

The rule of Predication maps (vii) into (viii):

(viii)

[the man]$_i$ [who$_i$ his$_i$ mother loved t_i best]

The representation (viii), an LF′ representation, then yields the interpretation (v).

Since the Bijection Principle applies only at LF, there is now no weak crossover violation in the case of (iii). In effect, *he* (of *his*) is associated with t in (iii) not at LF, which would yield a weak crossover violation, but only indirectly, by the rule identifying i and j that maps (vii) into (viii), thus treating *his mother loved* ____ *best* as an open sentence predicated of *the man*. Since no such analysis is possible for (iv), a weak crossover violation results if we attempt to interpret (iv) as (vi).

Thus, there is some evidence for a principle of relative clause interpretation involving a kind of predication, which we may think of as mapping LF representations into LF′ representations by identifying indices. Similar arguments apply to left dislocation (in English) and clefts, but not to the constructions discussed in the text that involve only a weaker "aboutness" relation between the topic and an associated clause (e.g. *as for John*, . . . , or such examples as (40) discussed in section 2).

Proceeding further, let us examine the properties of LF'. Edwin Williams has observed that the binding theory seems to apply to such representations. Thus, consider the left-dislocation structure (ix):

(ix)

John$_i$, he$_j$ likes him$_k$

Suppose that the Predication rule identifies i and k; thus, we take the open sentence in (ix) to be (x), predicated of *John*:

(x)

he likes ____

Then the representation at LF' is (xi):

(xi)

John$_i$, he$_j$ likes him$_i$

Suppose, however, that $i = j$ at LF (that is, in (ix)), so that the sentence (ix) is interpreted as (xii):

(xii)

for x = John, x likes x

However, (xii) is not a possible interpretation for (ix), even though (ix) satisfies all conditions that hold at D- or S-structure or at LF. It must be, then, that the binding theory rules out (xi) at LF', where $i = j$. Therefore, the binding theory holds at LF'.

There is good reason to suppose that the binding theory applies at S-structure (see Chomsky (1981a, chapter 3) and the discussion of (62) in section 4). If the binding theory applies at S-structure and at LF', then it is plausible to suppose that it also applies at LF, hence, at all syntactic levels apart from D-structure. Perhaps, then, something like the Projection Principle applies to the binding theory, as it does to θ-theory. In forthcoming work, Youssef Aoun provides considerable further evidence that the binding theory applies at LF and shows that on this assumption, we can derive major properties—perhaps all properties—of the ECP; see note 4. While this seems to me a plausible conclusion, I will put further consideration of it aside here.

Whether these suggestions concerning further representations beyond LF are right or wrong, they are subject to no methodological objections on grounds of Occam's razor or proliferation of grammars. What is at stake is the proper interpretation of relative clause constructions, and neither of the alternatives considered yields a greater variety of grammars or of principles. See also the next footnote.

Note incidentally that the barrier to vacuous operators, one element of a system of principles involving binding of operators and variables as noted, eliminates any motivation in terms of such examples as (7) for the proliferation of base rules and categories in enriched phrase structure grammars such as those proposed by Gazdar (1981). Gazdar argues that this enrichment is supported empirically by properties of constructions involving across-the-board deletion in the sense of Williams (1978), but this appears dubious. Without going into details, note that further devices and assumptions are required for this proposal to work; these amount to imposing a certain parallelism requirement (see note 31), and it seems that when this requirement is formulated in proper generality it yields essentially the same results without the proliferation of rules and categories. On this matter, which clearly deserves further discussion, see also George (1980).

12. See Berwick and Weinberg (1982), Chomsky (1981c). Some of the discussion of this topic appears to rest on the assumption that a theory with one "type of rule" is preferable on some general grounds of explanatory power, simplicity, relevance to language acquisition, or whatever, to a theory that makes use of a variety of devices. This is an illusion, however. Thus, it is well known that a theory that allows only one "rule type", namely, unrestricted rewriting rules, is essentially universal, but no one assumes that it is preferable on these grounds to a theory with more articulated mechanisms. The fallacy was at one time current with regard to "derivational constraints" (see Chomsky (1972, chapter 3), for discussion) and is now sometimes voiced with regard to phrase structure grammars, specifically, classes of such grammars equivalent in weak generative capacity to context-free grammars, or the latter class itself. As for this class, there is no reason to suppose that it bears any close resemblance to the class of grammars for possible human languages, and much reason to suppose that it does not; see Berwick and Weinberg (1982) for discussion. The crucial empirical question has to do not with generative capacity, number of "rule types", etc., but rather with limiting the variety of grammars that are readily available given restricted data (see Chomsky (1965, 62) and elsewhere). Highly modular systems face no particular problem in satisfying this requirement as compared with systems having a more uniform "rule type". One might in fact suspect that the contrary would prove to the be the case, if the question were put more clearly. Robert Berwick explores this question in forthcoming work.

13. Note that this principle does not exclude the possibility that certain verbs might take VP-complements lacking a subject position. Argument in favor of this proposal for one class of Romance causatives is presented in Burzio (1981), which shows that these possible V–VP constructions have quite different properties from raising or control structures.

14. See Chomsky (1981a, chapter 3) for discussion of various approaches to this question and of some extensions that I will ignore here; for a more comprehensive analysis of various options, see Sportiche and Aoun (1981). The approach they develop and defend differs from (13) in two basic respects: it deletes reference to c-command and replaces the final clause by the requirement that α and β share all maximal projections. They also suggest a revision of the notion of c-command: α c-commands β if and only if β appears in every maximal projection that contains α. Then government is a "symmetrized" version of c-command, with the added condition that the governor is a zero-order category of X-bar theory. Sportiche and Aoun appeal to a general principle barring representations of the form $[_i... [_i...] ...]$ to do the work of the addi-

tional requirement that α not dominate β in familiar definitions of "α c-commands β". This condition is also important in binding theory; see note 16. The general effect is that the head of a maximal projection governs exactly the categories that appear within this maximal projection and are not protected (in the sense of the text) by another maximal projection. These ideas have much to recommend them, but I will not pursue the issues raised in any detail here.

One crucial question left unresolved in these discussions is posed by constructions of the form (i):

(i)

$[_{VP*}[_{VP} \text{ V...}] \alpha]$

Here we may think of VP as a phrase containing V and its complements, and VP* as a phrase containing elements not subcategorized by V. The structure (i) may be base-generated, under certain assumptions about the constituent structure of clauses containing adjunct phrases. Or it may be formed by a transformational rule, for example, the NP Inversion rule in a pro-drop language that yields such structures as (ii):

(ii)

$e \; [_{VP*}[_{VP} \text{ parla}] \text{ Giovanni}]$
'Giovanni is speaking'

Here α of (i) is NP, moved from the subject position occupied by e in (ii). There is good reason to believe that NP in (ii) is governed, in fact properly governed, by the verb in (ii); namely, as Luigi Rizzi has pointed out, this NP is an extraction site, so that the ECP requires proper government. (See Rizzi (forthcoming).) On the other hand, there is no *ne*-cliticization from the NP position to the V in such constructions as (ii), which would seem strange if V governs this position. There are several possible ways of resolving the problem. One is to adopt the extended notion of c-command discussed in connection with (34), so that V governs α in (i), and to restrict *ne*-cliticization to constructions in which the source of *ne* is a thematic argument of V, with various modifications for more complex constructions. This approach can be accommodated straightforwardly within the theory of Sportiche and Aoun if we understand the relevant notion of "maximal projection" in their definitions to include VP* but not VP in (i), (ii).

15. On small clauses, see the discussion in Chomsky (1981a), following ideas of Tim Stowell, developed in turn from earlier work of Edwin Williams. Kayne (1981b) presents an interesting alternative to the S'-Deletion approach to Exceptional Case-marking, showing that it generalizes to other phenomena as well. See Chomsky (1981a, chapter 5) for a brief discussion. I will tentatively assume the S'-Deletion approach here, though little turns on the decision in the present context.

The Exceptional Case-marking structures appear to be marked cases, presumably learned by direct exposure to such examples as (14). In other languages, other devices are sometimes used to permit lexical subjects of infinitives by some kind of special Case-marking in this ungoverned position. Note that the process of S'-Deletion (or some equivalent) is generally available, as in (15), (16); there is good reason to suppose that such cases exist precisely because a process of "reduction" of major categories from maximal to nonmaximal projections is available. If so, then the device is available to the language learner and can therefore readily be employed in the marked case (14). We should expect marked constructions to tend to have this characteristic; that is, they should extend available devices, rather than adding completely new ones.

16. Actually, a somewhat different notion is required, which will eliminate reference to S and NP. See Chomsky (1981a, chapter 3). Among other consequences, this approach also correctly differentiates the behavior of NPs with and without subjects with respect to binding. I will put this matter aside here, however.

17. In work in progress, Aoun suggests that the binding theory should be extended to $\bar{A}$-binding. See notes 4 and 11.

18. But see note 17. If Aoun is correct, then a variable is an R-expression and an anaphor, in terms of the binding theory.

19. Assuming Subjacency, hence successive cyclic movement, the COMP in (30b) is [t $that$], where t is the trace of who. If $that$ is not present, the COMP is [t] and the embedded subject trace is governed, in fact properly governed, by the trace in COMP; this satisfies the ECP, so that $who\ do\ you\ think\ won$ is grammatical. Such devices as the French que-to-qui rule achieve the same effect. To explain the status of (30b), it is necessary to show that the trace subject of the embedded clause is not properly governed by an element in COMP, given the COMP [t $that$]. One possibility is that t does not c-command (and hence does not govern) the embedded subject trace in this case. If, however, we adopt the approach of Sportiche and Aoun discussed in note 14, this analysis is excluded, since t in COMP does c-command the embedded subject trace. We can then resort to the approach developed in Aoun, Hornstein, and Sportiche (1981), which they show to be well motivated on other grounds. Note that a slight modification of the notion of government is required for these analyses; see the references cited for details.

The question is somewhat peripheral to the main line of discussion here, so I will not pursue it. However, I will be tacitly assuming, following Sportiche and Aoun (1981), that an operator in COMP can serve as an $\bar{A}$-binder of a variable in the associated S even if the complementizer is present. Other assumptions are also quite compatible with the exposition that will follow, under slight modifications of various concepts and proposals. The matter should be clarified in a fuller exposition, but nothing of significance appears to hinge on it in the present context.

20. See, for example, Chomsky (1977; 1981a), Den Besten (1978), Milner (1978), Taraldsen (1978a), Van Riemsdijk (1978), Kayne and Pollock (1978), Rizzi (1980a), Torrego (1981). For differing views, see Christensen (1981), Engdahl (1981b), and many previous studies. I will return below to the alleged dis-

tinction between "bounded" and "unbounded" variants of what I am assuming here to be instances of Move α, and to the meaning of the latter concept.

21. Note that a variable is impossible in this position by virtue of the ECP:
(i)
*whose did John like [t winning the race]
This would then appear to be another example (like (30b)) in which the ECP for variables cannot be reduced to Case and θ-theory. It might be, however, that genitive Case is adjoined to NP and moved with NP under *Wh* Movement in (i), leaving t without Case, so that the θ-Criterion is violated under the Visibility Principle.

22. See Taraldsen (1978b). Note that in this case PRO does have independent, indeed definite, reference. In Chomsky (1981a), it is proposed that this definite PRO is distinguished from control PRO by the fact that it is governed by INFL at D-structure, a property carried through the derivation.

There have been a variety of approaches to what has been called the *pro-drop parameter* (I will keep to this familiar term here, though Rizzi's term *null subject parameter* is more perspicuous), including Jaeggli (1980), Rizzi (1980b), Burzio (1981), Chomsky (1981a), Napoli (1981), Safir (1981), Suñer (1981), Taraldsen (1981). I will return to this question in section 5.

23. Taraldsen (1981) exploits a similar idea in quite a different way in his approach to the pro-drop parameter. On the notions "c-command" and "government", see the references of note 14. Note that the relevant notion of "c-command" will not permit an element to c-command outside of the maximal projection of which it is the head; thus, an intransitive verb does not c-command the subject of the VP, even if there is no branching within the VP.

24. In (35a), one might argue that the antecedent of PRO is not *they* but rather an "implicit" *for*-NP complement to *difficult,* as Robert Fiengo suggests, recalling earlier treatments of "Super-Equi". This would then account for the fact that the example with the embedded infinitival subject is considerably less acceptable if *difficult* is replaced, say, by *prevented,* which does not take such a complement. (It is less clear to me, however, that the status of the example with the gerund subject is similarly degraded in acceptability as a result of this property of *prevented.*) Even under such an interpretation as this, (35b) would constitute a Subjacency violation, indeed one of the cases in which the antecedent of PRO need not c-command it.

Other apparent violations of Subjacency raise interesting questions. Consider for example (i) and (ii):
(i)
the men think that any attempt [PRO to feed each other] will be resisted
(ii)
the men think that any attempt [PRO to feed them] will be resisted
The antecedent of PRO in both cases appears to be *the men,* violating Subjacency. The conclusion is less than certain, however, as we can see by consid-

ering the understood subject of *attempt* in the two cases. In (i) we understand the subject of *attempt* to be *the men;* it is the men who are making the attempt. In (ii), however, if *them* is taken to refer to the men, then the subject of *attempt* must be other than *the men* (someone else is making the attempt); while if *them* is taken as free in reference, the subject of *attempt* may or may not be *the men*. Exactly these results would follow from the binding theory if *attempt* in these examples has a PRO subject, controlled by *the men* or arbitrary in reference (for example, if the structure of *any attempt* were something like *any (of) PRO's attempt* (analogous perhaps to *any of his attempts*)). In this case, control of the PRO subject of *feed* would not violate Subjacency.

These observations may bear on the major problem left unresolved by the version of the binding theory discussed in the reference of note 16 and by its predecessors, namely, that in the context (iii), anaphors as well as pronouns without disjoint reference may appear, as in (iv):

(iii)

[$_{NP}$ —— N']

(iv)

a. they like [each other's books]

b. they$_i$ like [their$_i$ books]

In general, pronouns have disjoint reference in the positions that admit anaphors. In the theory referred to above, which I am tacitly assuming here, (iva) is admitted and (ivb) excluded. A similar phenomenon has frequently been noted in context (v), where both cases of (vi) are more or less acceptable:

(v)

[$_{NP}$ Det N of ——]

(vi)

a. John heard [a story about himself]

b. John$_i$ heard [a story about him$_i$]

Again, the theory we are assuming accepts (via) but rejects (vib). Assuming that it is the status of (ivb), (vib) that requires explanation, we might conclude that what is involved is a special property of pronouns within NP. Notice, however, the quite different status of (vii):

(vii)

a. John$_i$ told [a story about him$_i$]

b. John$_i$ concocted [a story about him$_i$]

c. John$_i$ took [a picture of him$_i$]

As in the case of (i) and (ii), we understand the "subject" of *story* (*picture*) differently in (vib) and (vii); it is John's story (picture) in (vii) but someone else's story in (vib). This property appears to hold quite generally. If so, then we might assume that as in (i) and (ii), there may be a "hidden" pronominal element in the determiner position of (v), with the matrix verbs of (vii) requiring that it be controlled by the matrix subject, while the natural interpretation of (vib) is that it is not controlled. Then the examples of (vi), (vii) fall under the binding theory with no modification, leaving just (iii), (iv) to be explained. Note that we cannot require that this hidden pronominal element appear, since reflexives are permitted in the context of (v) independently of any interpretation of the "subject" of *story*.

These observations suggest that pronouns can (for some reason) be regarded as anaphors in the context (iii). This conclusion is supported by the well-known fact that there are necessarily bound pronouns in such idioms as (viii), but there are no corresponding cases such as (ix):

(viii)

John lost his way

(ix)

John took a picture of him

For further discussion, based on somewhat different assumptions about the (somewhat murky) facts, see Fiengo and Higginbotham (1981).

25. Recall that this property of PRO follows (in part) from the fact that PRO, like all pronominals, is subject to Principle B of the binding theory.

26. On anaphors having gaps as antecedents, see (24); also the later discussion of (64b). An example similar to (24) with *him* in place of *himself* illustrates that the gap must be present as a potential EC antecedent for a pronominal, by the binding theory; thus, in *the boy that he expected* [t *to hurt him*], *him* cannot be taken as the bound variable even under the resumptive pronoun strategy, though it need not be disjoint in reference from *he*, which immediately c-commands it in surface structure.

27. Note that the status of PRO and *each other* is reversed in the equivalent of (37a) in languages that lack the marked property of Exceptional Case-marking.

The complementary distribution is further illustrated in (34), contrasting with (i), and (32), contrasting with (ii):

(i)

 they like [each other's books]

(ii)

*they like [each other's winning the race]

Both (i) and (ii) raise questions. The problem in the case of (i) is that the position of the anaphor is not a position of disjoint reference; see note 24. The problem in the case of (ii) is that the position of the anaphor does not lack Case, so (ii) is not blocked by the Case Filter (and since the position is ungoverned, PRO is not blocked by binding theory, as in (32)). One possibility is that (ii) is barred by a rather obscure plurality requirement for English reciprocals (compare (i) with *they like [each other's book]). In this case, the equivalent of (ii) should be grammatical in a language lacking this requirement but admitting gerunds with subjects. Another possibility is that *each other* is indeed an anaphor at S-structure but is interpreted as a variable at LF, along lines suggested in Chomsky (1981a, 101). Then (ii) would be excluded at LF by the ECP, and the equivalent should be excluded even in languages lacking the plurality requirement.

Note that (i) and (ii) are barred by the version of the binding theory presented earlier, but admitted by the improved theory alluded to in notes 16 and 24.

28. The situation in fact is a bit more complex. In addition to the optionality of *for* at D- and hence S-structure, there is also an idiosyncratic rule of *For* Deletion in immediate postverbal position, dialectally variable and presumably part of the PF component, in the case of such verbs as *want, prefer*. See Chomsky (1981a).

29. The qualification "virtually" is necessary because trace must not only be governed, but properly governed, a narrower notion. Thus, there is one type of NP to which no gap corresponds, namely, a position that is governed (excluding PRO) but not properly governed (excluding trace). A possible example is the subject of an NP with a nominal head, as in (34). Since the subject position is governed, PRO is excluded; since it is not properly governed, trace is excluded as well (that is, **whose did you see book* is ruled out). However, see note 21.

30. For discussion of this topic, see Higginbotham (forthcoming). It appears that some version of Principle C remains, but that there is no reason to suppose it to be part of the binding theory or at least to bear on ECs.

There is some independent evidence supporting the conclusion that t' in (49) is not an $\bar{A}$-binder. Thus, it is natural to suppose that a category functions as an operator just in case it functions as an $\bar{A}$-binder. But it is clear that in (49) t' does not function as an operator, at least with regard to selectional properties of the matrix verb; thus, *think* does not subcategorize for a complement of the form operator-S, and in fact no verb subcategorizes for a complement of this form where the operator is an EC. Furthermore, as Youssef Aoun observes, there are weak crossover violations in such structures as (i) and (ii):

(i)

who did his mother think [t would win]

(ii)

who did the woman he loved think [Mary would marry t]

Compare (i) and (ii) with *his mother thought Bill would win, the woman he loved thought Mary would marry Bill*. If the weak crossover effect is explained by something like the Bijection Principle, then we do not want to take the EC in the COMP of the embedded structure to be an operator (hence an $\bar{A}$-binder), for this reason. Recall that a variable can be coindexed with an element outside of the scope of its $\bar{A}$-binder, as we have seen.

There are many further questions concerning the structure of the LF component to which these considerations are relevant. Note that we must assume the EC operator of (43) to be distinguishable from trace in COMP.

Notice that in such constructions as (iii), which we assume to have the S-structure and LF representation (iv), there is an empty operator rather than a *wh*-phrase in COMP:

(iii)

the book [that I read t]

(iv)

the book [$_{S'}$[$_{COMP}$ O_i that] [$_S$ I read t_i]]

Clearly t is a variable, so it must be $\bar{A}$-bound. One might imagine that it is $\bar{A}$-bound by the head of the NP, *the book*. This is probably not the case, however, for the reasons discussed briefly in note 11. Therefore, it is $\bar{A}$-bound by O, just as it is $\bar{A}$-bound by the overt operator in (v):

(v)

the book [which I read t]

Two conclusions follow. We must appeal to the doubly-filled COMP filter of Chomsky and Lasnik (1977) to exclude (vi), and we must assume that the internal branching in COMP in (iv) does not prevent binding of t by O:

(vi)

the book [which that I read t]

The latter conclusion suggests that we should adopt the notion of c-command and government, and the analysis of the *[*That*-Trace] Filter, proposed by Aoun, Hornstein, and Sportiche (1981), discussed briefly in notes 14 and 19. Again, other assumptions are compatible with the basic line of development of the argument here, but I will tentatively assume this to be correct.

31. I omit here the case of "across-the-board movement" in coordinate constructions, which Engdahl (1981a) shows to be a distinct phenomenon. If this phenomenon is interpreted as in Williams (1978), then the Bijection Principle must be relaxed for just this case. If it is interpreted as in George (1980), with parallel application of Move α in the coordinated phrases, then the Bijection Principle can be maintained for this case.

The discussion of (7), (8) is relevant here. Evidently, a property of parallelism is central to "across-the-board movement". Thus, paired objects and paired subjects can be deleted, as in (i), but not a paired subject and object, as in (ii):

(i)

a. a man who John likes and Bill hates

b. a man who likes John and hates Bill

(ii)

a man who John likes and hates Bill

As Williams has observed, however, the situation is more complex, since (iii) and (iv) are much more acceptable than (ii):

(iii)

a man who John likes and I think hates Bill

(iv)

a man who John likes and I have the impression hates Bill

Furthermore, there need not be a gap in the conjoined structures if the resumptive pronoun strategy is used; if used, however, it must be used in both structures, as in (v):

(v)

a man who a friend of his likes Bill and one of his brothers hates Tom

As in the case of (7), (8), we cannot say that paired gaps are required in surface form; rather, an LF parallel of some sort is involved. The problem is to find the uniform notion of LF parallelism that apparently underlies this phenomenon, a point that is clear in Williams's study, which initiated the investigation of this question.

32. Taraldsen derives the basic properties of parasitic gaps from the assumption that a Case-marked EC is a variable, rather than from the θ-Criterion and the functional determination of ECs, as below. This modification of Taraldsen's argument seems well motivated. In the first place, the assumption in question does not readily extend to exclude parasitic gaps licensed by NP-trace where the gap is not Case-marked, as for example in *John was killed t [before it was believed [e to be found]]. (There would be no binding theory violation here for reasons discussed in the reference of note 16, and Subjacency is irrelevant.) More generally, though, the status of the assumption that Case-marked EC is a variable is dubious. If the assumption is correct, we would expect it to follow from some more general principle. Nor is its descriptive accuracy beyond dispute; see references cited in Chomsky (1981a), as well as section 5 of this study, where it is explicitly rejected. Note that the converse assumption, that a variable is Case-marked, is well motivated both empirically and as a special case of the Visibility Principle discussed earlier and in Chomsky (1981a).

The concept "c-command" in (56), (58) requires some further discussion and refinement, exactly as it does with respect to the binding theory. See Engdahl (1981a) for discussion of this topic, which we ignore here; also Chomsky (1981a, chapter 3, note 37).

33. There might in fact be other traces in the chain. We ignore this possibility, which reduces to the same considerations reviewed here.

34. Engdahl makes a number of criticisms of the proposal in Chomsky and Lasnik (1977), but they are not really relevant since she does not distinguish A- from Ā-binding and does not consider the movement-to-COMP analysis for complex adjectival constructions. Nevertheless, I think that that proposal should now be rejected on the grounds discussed here.

35. A personal experience may be relevant. In Chomsky (1955), the example (i) is discussed as an example of a position from which wh-movement is impossible:

(i)

whom did your interest in t VP

In subsequent years this and similar examples motivated discussions of the A-over-A Condition and other proposals designed to determine the conditions governing movement rules. In lectures and discussions, I have frequently used such sentences as (ii) as examples:

(ii)

whom did your interest in *t* surprise Bill

Almost without exception, I found that I cited the example with a gap in place of *Bill*, then correcting it to the intended case, without understanding why. The reason is, of course, that (ii) is ungrammatical whereas replacement of *Bill* by *e* yields a more or less acceptable parasitic gap construction, irrelevant to the point I was attempting to make with (i) and (ii) but nevertheless much easier to say than (ii).

36. The following discussion diverges from the assumptions of Chomsky (1981a,b,c), which I have so far been following for the most part.

37. Strictly speaking, there could be such an element if it were restricted to positions that are assigned Case but not under government, e.g. perhaps in genitive constructions. Presumably, restriction of an element to just such positions is excluded.

38. The inherent feature content of arbitrary PRO is subject to language-specific variation. Thus, it is plural in Italian but singular in Spanish.

39. See Chomsky (1981b). Though I am now rejecting the approach to the pro-drop parameter outlined there and in Chomsky (1981a), for the reasons just discussed, some of the underlying assumptions appear plausible. Thus, it must be possible for INFL to be attached to the main verb at S-structure, as in the case of verb or verb phrase movement in the syntax.

40. We might ask whether the distribution of PRO can be explained on the assumption that Case-marked pronominals are pronouns, without appealing to binding theory. Thus, if *e* in (i) is assigned Case, then it will be spelled out as a pronoun and the construction will be barred by the Case Filter (failure of Case-checking), so that only PRO can appear here:

(i)

it is clear [what *e* to do *t*]

The question, then, is whether it is lack of Case or lack of government that determines the distribution of PRO. To answer it, we must consider constructions in which there is Case but no government, or government but no Case. Examples of the first type include, for example, the subject of gerunds, an ungoverned position that admits PRO or Case-marked lexical NP. One might argue, however, that such examples are not crucial on the grounds that Case is optional. This move is somewhat dubious, however, since if Case-assignment (or checking) is optional generally, then PRO lacking Case should be able to appear freely in positions where Case is assignable (e.g., object of a verb) if it is Case that determines whether an element is PRO or a pronoun. Furthermore, there appear to be fairly convincing examples, though not in English, where PRO must be Case-marked (though it remains ungoverned) to account for adjective agreement, so that it seems doubtful that one can maintain in general that PRO lacks Case. There is forthcoming work by Jane Simpson reviewing this matter.

Consider examples of the second type, where we find government but not Case. These would include, for example, such constructions as the following:

(ii)
a. there was killed *e*
b. it was persuaded *e* S'
c. the belief [*e* to be sad]
d. the sale *e* for profit   (compare "the sale of slaves for profit")
e. the sale for profit *e*

In such examples, *e* is governed and clearly cannot be PRO with arbitrary interpretation (there is no antecedent). If the distribution of PRO were determined by lack of Case, then PRO should be able to appear in these constructions. If one were to argue that somehow Case is assigned, blocking PRO, then a pronoun (e.g., *he*) should also be able to appear, as is not the case. In example (iid), one might argue that *of*-insertion is obligatory, but this is a dubious move. First, note that the same theory would have to assume that assignment of genitive Case to the subject is optional, to permit PRO subject of gerunds. Furthermore the rationale for the rule of *of*-insertion (namely that it permits lexical NP in positions determined by the Projection Principle but otherwise violating the Case Filter) would be lost. Optionality of the rule of *of*-insertion is also required by the "passive nominals" such as "the city's destruction" derived from the form "the destruction—the city" predicted by the Projection Principle and $\bar{X}$-bar theory; as has often been noted, this may be the correct analysis for expressions of the form NP'*s*-$\bar{\text{N}}$ in general. Finally, (iie) would still be unaccounted for since this is not a position of *of*-insertion. The same observation holds more generally, if adjacency is a condition for Case-assignment, in accordance with earlier discussion.

It seems, then, that the distribution of PRO is determined by lack of government, not lack of Case, though the two properties will often correlate. Lack of government follows from the binding theory if PRO is a pronominal anaphor, as we have seen. As was noted earlier, this assumption concerning the status of PRO is natural, both in terms of (104) and in terms of the quasi-semantic properties of PRO, which shares the basic properties of pronominals (it is either free or bound by an element with an independent θ-role) while sharing with anaphors the property of lacking independent reference (with the provisos mentioned concerning the notion of reference).

41. This phrase may be a clause (as in *it is clear that S,* e *è chiaro che S*) or an inverted NP, which may be base-generated in direct object position or adjoined to the VP by movement, as in (66). On this topic, see the extensive discussion in Burzio (1981) and the brief summary in Chomsky (1981a), based on work by Burzio (which in turn derives in part from ideas of David Perlmutter, Luigi Rizzi, and others).

42. Note that the approach just sketched makes it impossible to eliminate Principle C from the binding theory along the lines discussed in connection with (49). The reason is that the EC of (49) (= (i)) is now permitted to be governed as an instance of pure pronominal *pro:*

(i)

who$_i$ does he$_i$ think [t_i' [t_i likes Bill]]

Assuming, as above, that t' is not an $\overline{\text{A}}$-binder, then t is locally A-bound by *he* and is *pro* by our present assumptions. However, this yields a violation of the pro-drop parameter, so that (i) is still barred. Similarly, we derive the strong crossover effect in (ii) from the failure of determination of content for the EC:

(ii)

who$_i$ does he$_i$ think [t_i' [Mary saw t_i]]

Note that (i) and (ii) are also barred independently by the fact that *who* is a vacuous quantifier lacking a variable. We must, of course, exclude the interpretation of (i) which takes *he* to be a resumptive pronoun functioning, in effect, as a variable; presumably, if a pro-drop language did allow resumptive pronouns of this type, (i) would be grammatical without the EC t', with t base-generated as pure pronominal *pro*.

43. See particularly Marantz (1981); also Koster (1978) and subsequent papers. I suspect that this may also be true with regard to at least some parts of the recent work in relational and lexicalist grammar. On these topics, see again Marantz (1981).

44. If so, then generative semantics and recent theories that rely on extensive phrase structure rules have ventured even farther astray, each selecting and pursuing one of two erroneous directions.

References

Aoun, Y., N. Hornstein, and D. Sportiche (1981) "Some Aspects of Wide Scope Quantification," *Journal of Linguistic Research* 1, 69–95.

Baltin, M. (1978) *Toward a Theory of Movement Rules,* Doctoral dissertation, MIT, Cambridge, Massachusetts.

Belletti, A., L. Brandi, and L. Rizzi, eds. (forthcoming) *Theory of Markedness in Generative Grammar,* Proceedings of the 1979 GLOW conference, Scuola Normale Superiore, Pisa.

Berwick, R., and A. Weinberg (1982) "Parsing Efficiency, Computational Complexity, and the Evaluation of Grammatical Theories," *Linguistic Inquiry* 13, 165–191.

Besten, H. den (1978) "On the Presence and Absence of *Wh*-Elements in Dutch Comparatives," *Linguistic Inquiry* 9, 641–671.

Borer, H. (1981) *Parametric Variations in Clitic Constructions,* Doctoral dissertation, MIT, Cambridge, Massachusetts.

Bresnan, J., and J. Grimshaw (1978) "The Syntax of Free Relatives in English," *Linguistic Inquiry* 9, 331–391.

Burzio, L. (1981) *Intransitive Verbs and Italian Auxiliaries,* Doctoral dissertation, MIT, Cambridge, Massachusetts.

Chomsky, N. (1955) *The Logical Structure of Linguistic Theory,* Plenum, New York (1975).

Chomsky, N. (1965) *Aspects of the Theory of Syntax,* MIT Press, Cambridge, Massachusetts.

Chomsky, N. (1972) *Studies on Semantics in Generative Grammar,* Mouton, The Hague.

Chomsky, N. (1977) "On *Wh*-Movement," in P. Culicover, T. Wasow, and A. Akmajian, eds., *Formal Syntax,* Academic Press, New York.

Chomsky, N. (1980a) "On Binding," *Linguistic Inquiry* 11, 1–46.

Chomsky, N. (1980b) *Rules and Representations,* Columbia University Press, New York.

Chomsky, N. (1981a) *Lectures on Government and Binding,* Foris, Dordrecht.

Chomsky, N. (1981b) "A Note on Non-control PRO," *Journal of Linguistic Research* 1, 1–11.

Chomsky, N. (1981c) "Knowledge of Language: Its Elements and Origins," in H. C. Longuet-Higgins, J. Lyons, and D. E. Broadbent, eds., *The Psychological Mechanisms of Language,* joint symposium of the Royal Society and British Academy, London.

Chomsky, N., and H. Lasnik (1977) "Filters and Control," *Linguistic Inquiry* 8, 425–504.

Christensen, K. (1981) "Filler–Gap Patterns in Norwegian," in T. Fretheim and L. Hellan, eds.

Emonds, J. (1976) *A Transformational Approach to English Syntax,* Academic Press, New York.

Engdahl, E. (1981a) "Parasitic Gaps," paper presented at the University of Massachusetts, Amherst, January 1981, at Sloan Workshop on Processing of Unbounded Dependencies; to appear in *Linguistics and Philosophy.*

Engdahl, E. (1981b) "Multiple Gaps in English and Swedish," in T. Fretheim and L. Hellan, eds.

Evans, G. (1980) "Pronouns," *Linguistic Inquiry* 11, 337–362.

Fiengo, R., and J. Higginbotham (1981) "Opacity in NP," *Linguistic Analysis* 7, 395–421.

Freidin, R. (1978) "Cyclicity and the Theory of Grammar," *Linguistic Inquiry* 9, 519–549.

Fretheim, T., and L. Hellan, eds. (forthcoming) *Proceedings of the Sixth Scandinavian Conference of Linguistics,* Tapir Publishers, Trondheim.

Gazdar, G. (1981) "Unbounded Dependencies and Coordinate Structure," *Linguistic Inquiry* 2, 155–184.

George, L. (1980) *Analogical Generalizations of Natural Language Syntax,* Doctoral dissertation, MIT, Cambridge, Massachusetts.

Graffi, G. (1980) "'Universali di Greenberg' e grammatica generativa," *Lingua e Stile* 15, 371–387.

Heny, F. (1981) Introduction to F. Heny, ed., *Binding and Filtering,* Croom Helm, London.

Higginbotham, J. (forthcoming) *Logical Form: Structures and Interpretation.*

Horvath, J. (1980) "Movement in 'Logical Form'; Evidence from Hungarian," paper presented at the annual meeting of the Linguistic Society of America, December 1980.

Huang, J. (1980) "Move WH in a Language without *Wh*-Movement," mimeographed ms., MIT, Cambridge, Massachusetts.

Jaeggli, O. (1980) *On Some Phonologically-Null Elements in Syntax,* Doctoral dissertation, MIT, Cambridge, Massachusetts.

Kayne, R. (1975) *French Syntax: The Transformational Cycle,* MIT Press, Cambridge, Massachusetts.

Kayne, R. (1979) "Two Notes on the NIC," in A. Belletti, L. Brandi, and L. Rizzi, eds.

Kayne, R. (1981a) "ECP Extensions," *Linguistic Inquiry* 12, 93–133.

Kayne, R. (1981b) "On Certain Differences between French and English," *Linguistic Inquiry* 12, 349–371.

Kayne, R., and J.-Y. Pollock (1978) "Stylistic Inversion, Successive Cyclicity, and Move NP in French," *Linguistic Inquiry* 9, 595–621.

Koopman, H., and D. Sportiche (1981) "Variables and the Bijection Principle," paper presented at the 1981 GLOW conference, Göttingen.

Koster, J. (1978) *Locality Principles in Syntax,* Foris, Dordrecht.

Lasnik, H., and J. Kupin (1977) "A Restrictive Theory of Transformational Grammar," *Theoretical Linguistics* 4, 173–196.

Marantz, A. (1981) *On the Nature of Grammatical Relations,* Doctoral dissertation, MIT, Cambridge, Massachusetts.

Milner, J.-C. (1978) "Cyclicité successive, comparatives, et cross-over en français," *Linguistic Inquiry* 9, 673–693.

Napoli, D. (1981) "Subject Pronouns: The Pronominal System of Italian vs. French," in *Papers from the Seventeenth Regional Meeting of the Chicago Linguistic Society,* University of Chicago, Chicago, Illinois.

Reinhart, T. (1976) *The Syntactic Domain of Anaphora,* Doctoral dissertation, MIT, Cambridge, Massachusetts.

Riemsdijk, H. van (1978) "On the Diagnosis of *Wh*-Movement," in S. J. Keyser, ed., *Recent Transformational Studies in European Languages,* Linguistic Inquiry Monograph 3, MIT Press, Cambridge, Massachusetts.

Rizzi, L. (1980a) "Violations of the *Wh*-Island Constraint in Italian and the Subjacency Condition," *Journal of Italian Linguistics* 5, 157–195; to appear in L. Rizzi (forthcoming).

Rizzi, L. (1980b) "Negation, *Wh*-Movement and the Null Subject Parameter," mimeographed ms., Università della Calabria; to appear in L. Rizzi (forthcoming).

Rizzi, L. (1981) "Lexical Subjects in Infinitives: Government, Case and Binding," mimeographed ms., Università della Calabria; to appear in L. Rizzi (forthcoming).

Rizzi, L. (forthcoming) *Issues in Italian Syntax,* Foris, Dordrecht.

Rouveret, A., and J.-R. Vergnaud (1980) "Specifying Reference to the Subject," *Linguistic Inquiry* 11, 97–202.

Safir, K. (1981) "On the Status of Null Expletive Elements," mimeographed ms., MIT, Cambridge, Massachusetts.

Sportiche, D., and Y. Aoun (1981) "On the Formal Theory of Government," paper presented at the 1981 GLOW conference, Göttingen.

Steele, S., with A. Akmajian, R. Demers, E. Jelinek, C. Kitagawa, R. Oehrle, and T. Wasow (1981) *An Encyclopedia of AUX,* Linguistic Inquiry Monograph 5, MIT Press, Cambridge, Massachusetts.

Stowell, T. (1981) *Origins of Phrase Structure,* Doctoral dissertation, MIT, Cambridge, Massachusetts.

Suñer, M. (1981) "On Null Subjects," mimeographed ms., Cornell University, Ithaca, New York. (To appear in *Linguistic Analysis.*)

Taraldsen, T. (1978a) "The Scope of *Wh* Movement in Norwegian," *Linguistic Inquiry* 9, 623–640.

Taraldsen, T. (1978b) "On the NIC, Vacuous Application and the *That*-Trace Filter," mimeographed ms., MIT, Cambridge, Massachusetts; distributed by the Indiana University Linguistics Club, Bloomington, Indiana.

Taraldsen, T. (1979) "The Theoretical Interpretation of a Class of Marked Extractions," in A. Belletti, L. Brandi, and L. Rizzi, eds.

Taraldsen, T. (1981) "The Head of S in Germanic and Romance," to appear in T. Fretheim and L. Hellan, eds.

Torrego, E. (1981) "Spanish as a Pro-Drop Language," mimeographed ms., University of Massachusetts, Boston.

Williams, E. (1978) "Across-the-Board Rule Application," *Linguistic Inquiry* 9, 31–43.